ADVANCE PRAISE

"Being a mother can seem like the hardest job on the planet. But mothering while in a struggling relationship is even more painful. And we often model for our kids unhealthy relationships and marriages, and we feel helpless as a wife and mother. We try everything we know to give the relationship new life when it falls on rocky ground, but sometimes even our best efforts and intentions just don't work, and we find ourselves more disconnected than ever from our husbands. Sharon Pope's When Marriage Needs an Answer will give you the tools you need to begin to engage differently and potentially create real transformation in your relationship."

– Lisa Smith, *The Peaceful Parent,*
author and parent coach
https://thepeacefulparent.com

"Stop agonizing, take a breath, and READ THIS BOOK! It's time to get the clarity you need to feel good about moving forward with knowing you are doing

the right thing. I assure you, working with Sharon goes way beyond traditional therapy or marriage counseling. Sharon's unique tools and insights will naturally unfold, detangle, and ultimately change the trajectory of your life in an authentic and natural process. You will feel like you are getting back in touch with your own heart so that you can hear and know what is true for you and your life...without judgement and always through deep, compassionate honesty. Sometimes it'll feel easy and other times it'll feel tough, but you will get there and you will have the clarity that you seek."

– Dr. Sheila Dean, integrative medicine nutritionist and author
www.IFNAcademy.com

"You might say that I'm one of the lucky ones: I'm madly in love with my husband, crazy about my three kids, and doing the work I was born to do in this world! I know....I know....but here's what I can tell you: It's actually NOT luck. And I wasn't always this in love with my husband. In fact, I screamed divorce more times in the early stage of being married than I care to share. The truth is a marriage that works, that's filled with love and passion and genuine care for one another, doesn't come easy. The tools Sharon teaches are what I wish I would have had a decade ago...maybe it wouldn't have been so hard to find these answers and create

this life with my hubby. If you're struggling in your marriage, wondering if you can fix it or if the only answer is to leave it, this is your book. And if you want to kick sug-a and take back the control it has on you (and get the bod you've always wanted as the bonus) regardless of your age...I'm easy to find."
– Jenn Edden, CHHC, sugar addiction expert
and founder, Sugar Freedom Method
www.jecoaching.com

"When Marriage Needs an Answer will equip you with the tools you need to sustain love over the long haul, as well as simultaneously honor your decision to move on, if that's what you choose to do. There is nothing more personal than our closest and most intimate personal relationships, and sometimes those seem to be the most difficult to sustain - especially when life can be overwhelming and stressful. If you and your husband are hurting and confused about what to do next- and you feel like you've tried everything you know to try to make it better - this may just be the lifeline you've been looking for. I know Sharon personally and I appreciate her thoughtfulness, experience, and consideration no matter what the decision ends up being."
– Pleasance Silicki, author, *Delight: Eight Principles for Living with Joy and Ease*
https://lilomm.com/

"The women I work with – those in their Menopause Journey – find themselves re-evaluating every part of their lives. They rethink their professional, personal, emotional, physical, and even spiritual selves. And then, there is their marriage. Too often, they find that the man they thought they'd married is not the man they find across the breakfast table. No longer satisfied with the marriage they have, they find themselves at a crossroad. Is it possible to create the kind of loving, connected relationship that will serve both partners for the rest of their lives or is the right step to release the relationship and move forward without regret? This is the book that will help you find the clarity you need to move forward whatever your decision."

– Jeanne Andrus, The Menopause Guru
www.menopause.guru

"Sharon Pope is such a wise and beautiful soul and is incredibly gifted at helping people tackle whatever issues they're facing, and she can help you do the inner work so that you can either get a different result or get the clarity to take your next steps and leave the relationship as lovingly and gently as possible."

– Lucy Griffiths, video marketing and coaching for entrepreneurs
https://lucygriffiths.com/

"I know first-hand how Sharon's work can help you get clear about whether or not a marriage can (or should) be saved or if it's time to release it. I was in the middle of a debilitating diagnosis – and even after my husband had an affair – I was still questioning myself and not entirely clear how to move forward without losing my sanity in the process. Sharon helped me get clear on all of that and is what has inspired me to serve in the way that I do as a coach for those struggling with Lyme disease."
– Kimberley Quirk, Live Well Health Coaching

"Sharon tells the truth about contemporary relationships with grace, compassion, and clarity. She sheds light on the unconscious beliefs we live by and helps readers to transform marriage from what they believe it should be into what actually works for them in the real world. She gently shows readers how to use those concepts we may have heard of but perhaps never quite understood how to use - acceptance; active learning; forgiveness. She shows us why changing our thoughts around an incident or situation is not settling, but spiritually expansive. Her respect for the marriage bond and her understanding of the power of its privacy and intimacy is obvious as she leads readers to make their own decision about the *future of their marriage - consciously - and with love for themselves and the other. Sharon knows how to be happy and she shows readers how to get there, too, by embracing the opportunity to become more awakened through marriage - whether they choose to stay or to go."*

– Reverend Stephanie Wild, Psychic Medium
www.reverendwild.com

WHEN
Marriage
NEEDS AN
Answer

**THE DECISION TO FIX YOUR
STRUGGLING MARRIAGE OR LEAVE
WITHOUT REGRET**

SHARON POPE
MASTER LIFE COACH

When Marriage Needs an Answer
The Decision to Fix Your Struggling Marriage
or Leave Without Regret

Difference Press, Washington, D.C., USA

ISBN: 978-1-68309-254-4

Cover Design: Jennifer Stimson
Editing: Todd Hunter
Author's photo courtesy of: Christopher Keels Photography

DP
DIFFERENCE
PRESS

For D.
All my heart, for all my life.

TABLE OF CONTENTS

INTRODUCTION

"Maybe the journey isn't so much about becoming anything. Maybe it's about un-becoming everything that isn't really you, so you can be who you were meant to be in the first place."
– Paulo Coelho

My husband and I both have living wills, which means that if we become incapacitated and cannot express what we want for our medical care our wishes are stated in advance.

I do not want to be kept alive by a machine if that's all my life would ever be. The reality of death doesn't frighten me; the thought of only being half-alive or in constant pain, however, is a fate much worse than death in my opinion. My wishes are that if it looks like life support in perpetuity or constant pain, just release me peacefully and don't carry an ounce of guilt about the decision.

My husband also doesn't want to be kept alive indefinitely by a machine, but he's very clear that he wants every possible remedy attempted before that decision is made for him. He wants to turn over every stone and ensure that every possible solution is explored before choosing to take him off life support.

It's a subtle, but important distinction. I think the same is true for our marriages, which are also living, breathing, evolving things.

There are some people who are clearly okay with having a marriage on life support, merely existing together, but without any desire, joy, or connection present.

There are others who are not okay with having a marriage on life support and if it ever comes to that point, they will release the relationship.

And then there are those, for whom this book is written, that want to know they did everything they possibly could to attempt to fix the marriage before making the painful decision to walk away. After talking to thousands of women about their struggling and disconnected marriages, most can only have peace about a decision to end their marriages after they know that they have truly tried everything they can to make the relationship feel good again.

Not Taking the Decision Lightly

Cheryl was at the end of her rope in her marriage. Her husband had moved out several months ago and although he still came around and took care of her and what she needed done around the house, he clearly was not with her as a lover and partner and this was all very confusing for her. Cheryl was no slouch; she owned her own business and advised others on how to start their own integrative medical practice. She wanted to know how she had gotten here in her relationship and whether there was any hope of working it out with her husband or if the only answer was to release the relationship and move forward. This was her second marriage and it had lasted twenty-two years so she didn't take the decision lightly.

We'll call Cheryl's husband Mark for the sake of anonymity. Cheryl always felt like she was just barely scratching the surface with Mark. He never really let her into his heart or let her know what she was feeling. After the kids were grown and gone it was sort of like he left as well, he was not really present with Cheryl and not really at home when he was home. He was on his phone often, considering it a necessary evil of running two businesses. She felt him checking out of the relationship, but she didn't know how to turn the tide. She continued trying to express what she needed in the relationship, but never saw any changes on his part to attempt to meet those needs. Cheryl began to feel like Mark just didn't care; he was so wrapped-up in his own life and business that the relationship had become the last priority.

That might have been okay for Cheryl when the kids were young, but now when they had the time, money, and space for themselves as a couple, she wanted a true partner. And he had recently gotten a place downtown for himself. Even though they were still intimate, he would often get up and leave to head home afterward. That left her feeling empty, alone and used...even after all these years together.

Cheryl wasn't yet ready to say goodbye. Even though they had grown apart...even though they had been living apart for the last few months... even though all her girlfriends told her she deserved better. She still wasn't ready; she needed to know she had done everything she could before walking away.

The Empty-Nester Syndrome

According to Pew Research and U.S. Census Bureau data, the rate of divorces in mature marriages has nearly doubled for couples age 50 and over throughout the past 25 years. Additionally, a study by the American Association of Retired People suggest that two-thirds of the time it is the women in this age category asking for the divorce. It's no longer a guarantee that just because you've been together for 20 or 30 years that you will remain together for another 20, 30, or 40 years.

Women today are waking up in many ways in our society. They want a voice. They want equal pay. They want to be able to pursue their interests. They want to feel comfortable in their own skin. They want a loving, connected, and passionate relationship. And they're willing to make the necessary changes to have these things in their lives.

In Harriet Lerner's book, *The Dance of Intimacy*, she talks about how the health of the relationship has traditionally been women's work. It's a broad brushstroke, for sure, but there's truth to what she says. Men have been taught to achieve, tending to reach for the next accomplishment. Once married, they may no longer try as hard to "win her love" as they once did...turning their gaze and attention toward a different goal in their life. Whereas women are the nurturers, so when the relationship starts to deteriorate, it is often the woman that takes notice and attempts to fix it.

It shouldn't be that way. It doesn't have to be that way. But research proves this to be true in the majority of relationships. I've seen this to be the case in my own relationship coaching practice.

Every marriage struggles occasionally and certainly there are some marriages that have seen more than their fair share of struggles. But the struggles in a marriage when you're a few years into the relationship look and feel very different than the struggles after spending a few decades together and raising children together:

- By now, you know everything there is to know about one another (or at least you think you do)
- You've had some of the same arguments multiple times (maybe even hundreds of times)
- The days of passion and excitement have been replaced by consistency and stability (right when we finally have time and energy left at the end of the day to finally feel passion)

Many people find me when their children are in high school, getting ready to graduate within a few years and needing Mom and Dad less and less. We can no longer throw ourselves into our children's lives to avoid facing the problems in our marriages. And we begin to think about what life will be like when the kids are grown and gone and it's just the two of us, staring across the table at someone who seems so known, and yet so far away.

Marriage 2.0

Maybe at some point in the midst of this struggle you wished you could turn the clock back to who you and your husband were as a couple when you first met, when everything was new and exciting, when you were still learning about one another and feeling butterflies when you kissed. But now, decades later, you are not that same person you were so long ago and your partner is not the same either. You're not the same woman you were in your twenties. You're not the same woman you were before you brought children into the world. You're not the same woman you were before you felt the loss, grief, and heartbreak that life will occasionally bring. Trying to turn back the clock on the relationship and be who you were when you first met is not an option.

Likewise, where you've been together as a couple recently isn't working, otherwise the marriage wouldn't be struggling and you wouldn't feel so disconnected and lonely. We know what the current version of the marriage looks like and feels like, so remaining in this place and enduring the relationship as it is today isn't a real option either.

If there is no going back to who you were, and where you are now isn't working, then the only logical answer is to move forward and create something new together. This is the 2.0 version of your marriage, the more aware version, the more evolved version, the version of you showing up as your best self within the relationship. The version that knows and accepts one another unconditionally. The version of the two individuals in the relationship that are emotionally more mature, more self-aware, and more engaged than ever before.

Just like Apple comes out with a new version of their iPhone every six months or so, each one with more functionality than before, it's time to upgrade your relationship and begin applying new concepts, insights, and functionality to the oldest institution we have so that we can start doing marriage differently and begin having greater success.

We Were All Ill-Equipped

We come into our most important, most intimate relationship without many tools to do it well. If we were learning to be an accountant, we would have some training to be proficient and effective. If we were going to be a speaker or writer, we would have some training in order to do it well. If we were going to be a coach of any kind, we would have not only our personal experience, but also the training needed to help our clients be successful.

The training for most of our relationships is built almost entirely on the very shaky foundation of what we saw and experienced at home growing up. We learned what love and marriage are supposed to look like based upon what our parents actively demonstrated for us. Unfortunately, they didn't have any training either.

I grew up in a home with parents that chose to stay together for the long haul, even when things became difficult. My brother and I had a large extended family with lots of aunts and uncles, both of my parents being the oldest in each of their large families, almost all of whom were Catholic. Much like my parents' relationship, all of my aunts and uncles entered into good, solid, steadfast marriages with good, solid, kind people. My grandfather (my dad's father) was the only one that seemed to struggle with marriage, having married and divorced many times after becoming a widower when my grandmother died far too young. He was the outlier, while the rest of the family made love and marriage look almost effortless.

What I learned growing up was that marriage was forever. I learned that marriage was primarily about commitment – commitment to one another and to the family.

I also learned some other things about what love and marriage were not:

They were not about connection or affection. I never saw my parents hold hands, kiss, or playfully pat one another on the behind while passing in the kitchen (like they do now, by the way).

They were not about expressing their love for one another verbally. I'm sure there were times when the words "I love you" were spoken by my parents to one another in front of us kids, but I don't recall them in my memory.

I was a witness to the quiet and abiding love between my parents as a couple, but I don't recall seeing it displayed or spoken. It was more of a silent and private understanding between them, rather than an expression that others could see and experience.

Not surprisingly, my first marriage was about making the right choice in a partner – the good guy, the nice guy, the safe and stable guy. I married the man a mother would absolutely choose for her daughter; the same kind of good, kind human being that my families chose for their own relationships.

This marriage, also not surprisingly, was not about affection or connection. We didn't touch or hold hands, unless of course sex was involved, but even that felt awkward and like something that I should do, rather than something that I wanted to do or desired for myself. This fit nicely with my good girl Catholic upbringing.

We didn't say "I love you" very often.

We weren't affectionate toward one another.

I recall asking my husband to give me a hug at least once each day. I had to add further clarification to that request – it needed to be a two-hand hug – when he kept giving me one-arm hugs standing next to me rather than in front of me. You would have thought we were childhood buddies or brother and sister if you didn't know that we were married.

We would sleep on opposite sides of a massive king sized bed, inches away but feeling miles apart.

This marriage looked picture-perfect from the outside, but felt empty and lonely inside.

I thought this was just how marriage was supposed to be. After all, it didn't look dramatically different than what I had seen growing up.

But Wait, There's More....

There was another important and pivotal lesson I learned growing up about being a woman inside of a marriage that impacted the way I showed up later in my own marriage. I learned that I needed to be a strong, independent woman and to never need a man to take care of me. That sounds like a good thing, until it comes to being able to be soft, open, trusting, and vulnerable in an intimate relationship.

My dad always struggled professionally, moving from one job to the next, and with each job change typically came a move, financial uncertainty, new schools, and new friendships to be formed. My mom had always been the quiet, strong, steady, and stable one, who eventually came into her own professionally and became the primary breadwinner for the family. There were many years where I knew she was holding the family together financially and even when she hated her job, she never quit.

Although completely unintentional by my parents, what I learned from that experience was to not rely on anyone else financially – even inside of a marriage – and to take responsibility for my own success. Don't get me wrong, this has served me well in many areas of my life. I had an impressive and successful corporate career before becoming a Relationship Coach. I'm now a successful entrepreneur, and throughout my life and my relationships, I've always made more money than my partner. That's not a coincidence and it's not something that's a part of my DNA. It's what I learned growing up in my family.

But being a strong and independent woman who doesn't have to rely on a man for anything has not always served me when it comes to relationships. After all, our marriages are partnerships, where we're supposed to help one another carry the emotional and physical weight of life. So bringing that "I don't need anyone for anything" energy to my intimate relationships wasn't creating space for my partner to support me and have my back. It certainly didn't provide space for an equal partner to stand beside me (money can create an unintentional hierarchy within the relationship). Sometimes I never stopped moving long enough to let myself be fully seen or known. And it did not allow me to soften, trust, and make myself vulnerable to my husband in the relationship. So, in that environment, how exactly were we supposed to create connection and intimacy?

I built a wall around myself and my heart inside that relationship. Funny thing about a wall is that, although we might feel safe back there by keeping others out, we create our own self-imposed loneliness.

If I Knew Then What I Know Now

I wasn't a relationship coach during my first marriage, but rather a hard-driving corporate executive and I didn't have any of these tools that I'm going to teach you in this book. So it's fair to say that I walked away from that marriage not having tried everything I could to make it work. I tried everything I knew at that time, but there was so much I didn't know, so much that I never learned.

I am often asked, "If you knew then what you know now, do you think you could have made it work with your first husband?" It's a difficult question for me to answer. The short answer is yes. The longer answer is, although I could have made it work and been fine, I still do not think I would have chosen to remain in the marriage. I've never been fine with "fine." I think the longings of our hearts don't become quieter with age, they become louder and louder until we finally begin to give them the space and attention they deserve. For me that was a closeness, a connection in my most intimate relationship that I am not convinced my first husband and I could have created together.

I had to have this exact experience for me to have the answers and insights and the relationship I do today. I had to be brought to that place of needing new answers so that I could find my way. Without these experiences, I never would have discovered Martha Beck's coaching programs. Without these experiences, I never would have found all the teachers that inspire me today, who bring me closer to the truth. Without these experiences, I would not be the woman I am today, serving in the way that I do to help women come to their answer for their hearts and their lives. I know that it was all divinely orchestrated.

This Will Save Something

I have a belief that we're all doing the best we can at any given time. My ex-husband did the best he could. I am doing the best I can each day. You are. Your partner is. Our parents were doing their best as well. We're doing the best we can even when we disappoint others and especially when we might disappoint ourselves.

Often when there's guilt about an action or a decision made, we can beat ourselves up pretty badly. We might even think, "I know better." Although we might know intellectually between good and bad, right, and wrong, that doesn't mean that we don't make choices from a place of fear or pain in the moment. And when others hurt us, disappoint us, or don't meet our expectations, we can feel hurt or anger about their choices. But when you realize that only hurting people take actions that intentionally hurt other people and we're all doing the best we can, it's so much easier to quickly forgive making choices that are free from fear and pain, honoring both ourselves and others.

There's so much that we do not know. And we never really know what we don't know until we learn it later and look back in hindsight. I never learned that it's okay to be openly affectionate with one another. I never learned that I can allow others to take care of me without it meaning I'm somehow weak. Most young boys learn to not express emotion, otherwise they'll never "be a man." Those young boys turn into grown men who don't know how to connect or express emotions. Girls are taught to be nice and accommodating so we often over-give and find plenty of people that are glad to over-take. We're also not taught how to set healthy and loving boundaries for ourselves, expressing preferences and opinions, whereas those very things were a sign of strength in boys. We learn what our parents have to teach us (with no relationship training of their own) and then we learn what society, culture, and religion would teach us, which is almost universally interpreted through the eyes of fear, scarcity, and control. We look around and see how most other couples aren't terribly happy or connected and assume this is simply how it is, although we watch the Hallmark movies and our hearts quietly ache for more.

We think love should feel effortless, but that's a fairy tale. Then we get married and find out that love is hard work until death do us part, but that feels like a prison sentence. What I want to offer is the awareness and understanding that there are tools available to you to help you create the kind of relationships that feel good to your soul, if you're willing to try with an open and loving heart. And if you genuinely apply the tools I'm going to teach you in this book, and the marriage still doesn't feel good, then you can walk away knowing you truly did everything you could before making the painful decision to leave. That's how you can either fix your marriage or move forward without regret and years of second-guessing.

Nearly a decade after my first marriage ended, I am now remarried and madly in love with my husband. He's a completely different person than my first husband, but honestly, I am a completely different woman than who I was back then. We are both equal partners and intimate lovers, able to be fully ourselves, knowing that we will always be loved unconditionally and fully accepted. The tools I share within this book are what I use in my own relationship. These are the tools I teach my private coaching clients. These are the tools that might just be the thing that save your marriage. But even if they don't save the relationship, they will absolutely save your life and your sanity, giving you an opportunity to love again in an entirely new way.

An Unlearning

In addition to simply never being equipped to be successful at relationships, we also have learned some things that hamstring our relationships from the start that we would do well to unlearn.

For many of us, it still feels like getting married is a goal to achieve, an accomplishment of sorts. We've found the right one and he chooses us (and we choose him). We decide to get married, and there's a lot of anticipation and excitement that comes along with that.

Sometimes we have quiet doubts leading up to the wedding that we never gave ourselves permission to voice. Or we did voice the concerns, and someone talked us out of them. Still, there was a hopefulness that things would work out and somehow be fine. We let internal – or external – dialogue speak louder than the quiet questioning in our souls.

Once we're married, we feel like we've accomplished the first major life goal and can move through the game of life and onto greater accomplishments like purchasing a home, finishing our degrees, solidifying our careers, and having children.

We often operate on stress and fumes as we achieve at work, reaching for greater and greater success each in our own way.

We construct a space that feels like home, bringing together parts and pieces from each of our lives, as well as some new additions that represent who we are as a couple together. We still have his favorite chair and our grandmother's wooden chest. We buy new master bedroom furniture and sometimes a dog or cat to try our hands at being responsible for something other than just ourselves.

At some point, we begin creating a family together and bring new life into the world. The moment a woman becomes a mother, she is told either directly or indirectly that her dreams and desires are now secondary – at least for the next several decades – and she's glad to do it. Both of you come to know a love for that child that you've never felt before – as though your heart just tripled in size. So you slowly but surely pour all you time, attention, love, and energy into this little human being. Midnight feedings lead to kindergarten and play dates, which then lead to elementary school and birthday parties. The kids need your help shuttling them between multiple activities, meeting increasingly higher expectations at school, and remaining safe in a hyper-connected and sometimes unsafe world.

Maintaining all of that, on any given day, leaves very little energy remaining for nurturing the relationship with our spouse. We're completely exhausted at the end of most days, falling asleep almost as fast as our heads hit the pillow.

We stop making deposits into the relationship.

We stop courting one another.

We stop being curious about one another, assuming we know everything there is to know by now.

And we place the relationship essentially on a shelf off to the side, while our time, love, focus, and energy is funneled elsewhere – naively assuming the marriage will take care of itself.

We've been taught that love is all we need to sustain the marriage. But love alone without any real investment or attention causes a slow, steady deterioration of our connection to one another. And because it happens so gradually over the course of years or decades, the disconnection that occurs often goes unnoticed until the gap between the two of you feels almost too far to bridge. And it becomes increasingly apparent as the children grow older and more independent, needing us less and less. We begin to think about what life will be like when the children are grown and gone and the only descriptive word that comes to mind is "roommates."

In order for our marriages to not become so disconnected, we need to unlearn:

A marriage isn't a goal to be achieved or a box to be checked off in our life path, but an ongoing symbol of commitment and love between two people.

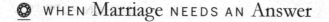

When we consciously poured our attention into what was next to accomplish, we unconsciously stopped pouring our love and focus into our marriages.

And nothing thrives while left unattended.

Tending the Garden

There is not a single thing on this planet that thrives when it is not tended to in some way. Plants that go without water and sunlight do not thrive. Children that go without love and acceptance do not thrive. Even a home that is uninhabited and not tended to deteriorates much more quickly than a home that has love and attention poured into it.

Think of your relationship as a garden. You plant seeds on the day you commit to one another. But if it never gets watered, if it never sees the sun, and if it's never pruned and weeded, how is it that you can expect it to thrive and bear fruit? We would never just throw some seeds on the hard ground, turn our backs to the garden for years and come back expecting it to be in full bloom...and yet, this is essentially what we do in our marriages.

It shouldn't be a surprise – although it usually is – when we grow further and further apart over the years when we don't tend to the garden of the relationship. We never think it will happen to us. And what's more, we don't know how it ever got this far, surprised by how it ever became this bad. It occurred so gradually over the course of years or decades that we didn't notice.

We began to feel a bit like roommates, but assumed it was just because our lives had become so busy; it will get better.

We didn't pay much attention when we began having sex less and less frequently, hoping that it's just a phase.

We felt increasingly alone and that caused us to be more irritated and less loving with one another, the resentments increased and so did the distance between us.

We explained away the small pains and told ourselves, "It will get better," still assuming the garden will grow on its own without much effort or attention.

We tried date nights, but that didn't work. Mostly, we sat there in silence, which only highlighted the distance between us.

We went to counseling a few times, but that just felt like rehashing the same issues over and over again.

We wait and wait thinking time will magically make the relationship better, but as we perpetuate the same arguments, the resentments increase, as does the distance between us.

When our relationship finally gets our attention, unfortunately it's at the point where it has become really painful – when the heartbreak is both wide and deep, or there's an affair, or there are words said or actions taken that can't be undone, or one of you moves out of the family home. Your relationship has your attention but you fear it may be too far gone to ever repair.

It's a shame that we wait until we're in despair to truly prioritize something, but this is unfortunately normal human behavior. We could learn and grow from a place of joy and contentment, always wanting to create a better version of ourselves and our relationships, but we rarely do. It's the seduction of the idea of hitting rock bottom. Change is difficult and growth feels like work, so we avoid it until it becomes unavoidable.

By the time we seek help with the relationship, it's beyond painful and on the brink of despair. If that's where you are right now, you don't have to give up hope, but hope will require something of you. It will require you to show up differently in your relationship, to engage it differently. It will require you to try and fail many times. And when you're willing to tell yourself the absolute truth, hope is right there on the horizon.

The Options for When a Marriage Is Struggling

Not only do we bring our experiences from growing up into our relationships, we also each bring with us the past traumas, the lessons learned growing up, the expectations others had of us, the baggage or hurts from past relationships, and our fears and insecurities, as well as dreams and desires; but, again, no real tools or training. It's not surprising that we have divorce rates hovering around 50% (these rates are much higher for second and third marriages) and an extremely high percentage of people who stay in unhappy relationships, but never actually divorce.

But what do you do when your best isn't working and the relationship is still struggling? Most people assume that this leaves you with only two options, neither of which feels even remotely possible: Either learn to endure the relationship as it is or throw in the towel and walk away.

Option 1: Staying and enduring the relationship as it is means giving up on happiness, never feeling seen or heard, appreciated or important. It might mean feeling alone and lonely even though you're in a relationship. It might mean – as it has for some of my clients – never being held or kissed or made love to again.

How do you consciously make that choice? Only when the alternative is even scarier:

Option 2: You could leave the relationship, blow up your life, dramatically impact your lifestyle, and lose friendships. You will be judged, maybe even by people that you love dearly. You tell yourself that such a decision will surely tear apart your family, hurt your children, and that you will most certainly grow old alone. Maybe some of this sounds familiar:

How could I ever do this on my own? Will I have enough money? Where will I live?

What if I hurt my children? What if they never speak to me again?

What will others think? Surely, they'll judge me. They'll never understand.

What if this crushes him? What if he never recovers? I don't want to hurt him.

What if I'm alone forever? Maybe this is better than being alone...

That also feels like an impossible choice.

This is where paralysis of the stay or go decision sets in because we believe there are no

good options. We don't know how to stay and we don't know how to leave either. So we choose to not make a decision and therefore unintentionally remain stuck in the pain, allowing the relationship to continue to deteriorate over time.

There is an alternative: You could dive into the marriage, applying all the tools you will learn in this book to genuinely see if something new can be created between you and your partner, something that feels so much better, something that works for both of you.

If you give it your all, consistently applying all the tools and it still doesn't work between the two of you, then you know you can move forward without second-guessing yourself and without years of regret. That's how you can open up two even more appealing options:

Option 3: Create the 2.0 version of your marriage together, one where you both feel connected and loving toward one another.

Option 4: Make the decision, after giving it your very best shot, to leave the relationship as gently, peacefully, and even as lovingly as possible. And when you choose to open your heart to love again, you'll be so much better equipped to create the kind of relationship that you both desire and deserve.

Options 3 and 4 are infinitely better options than staying and enduring or walking away in pain.

Don't fall into the trap of choosing either options 1 or 2. Both of those will keep you unhappy and feeling stuck. Staying in a marriage where you feel empty and alone is a terrible option, as is blowing up your life and storming out of a marriage, leaving a trail of hurt and pain in your wake.

Instead, use this book and the tools within it to help you choose between options 3 and 4.

How Do We Move Forward?

Now that we know how we got to this place of intense struggle in our marriages (no training in how to do relationships well and so many things we need to unlearn), it may be surprising that anyone is happily married these days. If anything else had a 50% plus failure rate, we would likely steer clear of it.

But we are human beings and as such, we're wired for human connection. We need one another in this life. I believe we are here to love and to be loved. I believe we need connection and relationships with each other, so even when the statistics might warn otherwise, we will always take a risk in love again and again and again.

As you move through the tools and ideas in this book, I ask that you remain open-minded.

Dr. Wayne Dyer said in one of his teachings that we all come into this world as soft and pliable, but we leave this world stiff and straight. Therefore, life is found in what remains soft but death is found in what remains hardened. If you remain hardened in the way you approach your relationship – insisting to do it your way, the way you've always done it, you should absolutely expect to continue to get the same results. However, if you soften and open your mind to new ways of engaging, new ways of showing up for your relationship, new life can be created, and new possibilities can exist.

Reading Is Not Enough

When you're in a great deal of pain, it's logical to seek answers. And sometimes, women will go from one article to the next, consuming one book after another, and investing in one course after another – each time thinking they will find the hidden answer that's been eluding them.

There's an enormous difference between passive learning and active learning. Passive learning is what we do when we're seeking information, when we're reading books or consuming article after article. Passive learning doesn't change anything in our relationships, it just makes us a little smarter. I could read a book about weight loss and at the end of that book, I know a little bit more but I haven't yet lost twenty pounds.

Active learning is when we take what we've learned and apply it to our lives and our relationships. Active learning is where all the change and growth occurs.

If you only read about how to do relationships differently, but never practice it, never apply what you've learned, you may know more about how relationships could work better at an intellectual level, but nothing will truly change in your relationship.

So I am telling you this – as an author myself – if you apply nothing you learn in this book, nothing will ever change. But if you apply what you learn – over and over and over again – you will get to an answer that you can trust and not second-guess.

Be Willing to Fail

Let's say you wanted to learn to play the piano. You read a book about how to read sheet music and you watched a few YouTube videos. You even began applying what you'd learned by sitting down at the piano regularly. At first, what you played didn't exactly sound like music and it felt really difficult. But the more you practiced, the better it sounded and the easier it became. You understood that practice was part of the learning and growth process.

You're going to learn some new tools, and of course, I'm going to ask you to apply them. It might feel difficult at first because you're learning a new skill, but with more practice, it will begin to feel easier.

As you apply these tools, they may not always work the first time. Just like the first time you sit down at the piano, what you play won't necessarily sound like music, neither will these tools work perfectly the first time you attempt to incorporate them. The whole time you're practicing the tools, to become better at using them, you're not failing. You're practicing. You're learning.

Good to Know

As you apply what you're learning, you will shift how you're showing up inside the relationship. You may react or respond differently than you normally do, you may not be as quick to criticize, and you may set new boundaries and new rules about what's okay with you and what's not okay with you. With every shift you make, your husband will likely notice and shift as well. He may not be conscious of it, but it's like a dance between two partners. You've been doing the salsa for years, so when you start doing the tango, he's likely going to notice. As he becomes more aware, he's going to give you information back and it's all – my three favorite words – good to know.

He will be giving you information all the time about what he's capable of being in the relationship and what he's not. This is information that is good to know.

He could respond to the changes with either curiosity or anger. This is information that is good to know.

You're going to see how you feel as you try these new methods and that is also good information to know.

It's not a test, but as you start showing up in the relationship as a woman you're proud of being, he will either rise to the occasion and meet you there at that new place or he won't. He gets a choice in this too. And it's all good to know.

The Decision Methodology

Have you ever been driving on the highway and veered off the road ever so slightly, only to hit the rumble strip? Those bumps or grooves in the pavement are there to alert you if you begin to veer off the road so that you can course-correct before you end up in the ditch. Your marriage likely hit the rumble strip years ago. You may have assumed it was a simple phase and ignored the warning signs, only to stand by while the relationship became worse, not better. And now the marriage is headed for the ditch. You have no choice but to pay attention.

No one reaches out to me when things are going well in their marriages. As a matter of fact, by the time women reach out for help and are willing to do this level of work, things are beyond bad in the marriage and at least one of the parties has a foot out the door. Sometimes it's too late and the disconnection between the two people is simply too far to bridge. But sometimes it's not. And the only way to know for sure is to try.

The methodology I'll be sharing with you through this work is to help you lean into your relationship again, putting forth your very best effort to see if something new can be created between you and your husband. As you change the way you engage, his reaction and responses to you will also likely change.

You've been trying what you know for creating change in your relationship and it hasn't worked because that's what brought you here. If you keep doing the same thing, you should expect to get the same result. So, I'm going to ask you to do it differently, to put your very best effort into creating change within the relationship by first changing how you're showing up in the relationship. We can only ever change ourselves, so that's where we have to begin.

And if you give it your very best effort and it still doesn't feel good, then you can walk away from the marriage and move forward without regret or years of second-guessing yourself about whether or not you made the right decision. This is the path we'll take to getting you the clarity you need to know whether you should stay or go.

The most difficult questions in our lives never have easy, simple answers. If sustaining healthy and loving relationships over the course of decades could be solved through three quick and easy steps described in a 1,000 word article, we wouldn't have the divorce rate we do today. They may not be quick and easy, but there are answers.

And I'm going to share with you my best tools so you can apply them to your life and your marriage and get the answers you're seeking.

Remain soft. Remain open. Go beyond just reading the concepts and really apply them in your life and your relationship. Be willing to keep trying what you learn here consistently until you begin to feel a shift, until it begins to sound like music. Know that all along the way as you apply these tools, you'll be getting information back from your partner that is all good to know.

I appreciate the trust you've placed in me. Let's get started.

STEP ONE:
A BASIS OF UNDERSTANDING

"We think our job as humans is to avoid pain, our job as parents is to protect our children from pain, and our job as friends is to fix each other's pain. Maybe that's why we all feel like failures so often - because we all have the wrong job description for love."
– Glennon Doyle Melton

Before we can dive into pragmatic tools to help you in your relationship, we first have to have a basis of understanding about the way our minds work, because it has been a key influencer in how you arrived at this place of struggle in your relationship.

I am no neurosurgeon, but I do understand the power of that which exists between our ears. Our brains are the most powerful and precious thing each of us have. You cannot exist without a brain and almost no amount of money can purchase a brain. Yet we pay precious little attention to it, take for granted its unique ability to learn and apply concepts.

You will hear me use the term "brain," as well as "the mind." Although they are related, those terms are not synonymous with one another. When I'm speaking about the brain, it will be a very specific region of the brain, the literal functioning of the tissues that make up the brain and how that relates to our actions and choices we make in our relationships. However, when I'm speaking about the mind, I'm talking about the broader sense of all that occurs beyond the basic workings of the brain. I'm talking about thoughts, feelings, attitudes, beliefs, inspiration, and imagination. I'm referring to thinking, judgement, memory, reasoning, and consciousness.

By the end of this section, you will have a very clear understanding of the role of the mind in the context of our most important and most intimate relationships. If your relationship is a bus, metaphorically speaking, then your mind has been the driver of that bus whether you realize it or not. If you're unaware or not paying attention, it may take you to some parts of town where you don't want to be, leaving you wondering how you got there and how to find your way back home. But if you become aware and learn how to better manage the mind, you can guide your driver to take you anywhere you want to go – including to the place where your struggling marriage feels peaceful and loving again.

The Clean Slate and How We Learn

We come into this world as essentially a clean slate. Our thoughts are as simple as "I'm cold! I'm hungry! I'm uncomfortable!" all being expressed through the only language we know at that time, crying out. But from the moment we're born, we are learning. We learn through our environment, our parents, the people around us, and by how different conditions make us feel.

A child's cerebral cortex, where all learning and reasoning take place, expands rapidly. It is why they're like little sponges, able to absorb, learn and recall information and experiences at astounding rates, repeating back to you the swear word you said and using it in the precise context and tone necessary to make a point. It's how the little ones can easily learn multiple languages and even bounce back and forth between them with ease. A child's ability to simply observe and absorb what they see is why "do as I say, but not as I do" has never worked.

As we grow older, there are more and more people influencing what we learn: family, friends, teachers, coaches, and people we look up to. We learn through society, television, movies, social media, the Internet, and advertising. Girls learn about how they should look to be loved and adored. Young boys learn how to behave to be considered "a man."

We are bombarded with millions of bits of data every second from all around us. We are limited by what we can pay attention to, so most of it simply gets tucked away as unconscious programming in our minds. And as we grow older and the pre-frontal cortex of our brains mature, we begin to settle into a more fixed way of thinking, and learning new things (like multiple languages) is more difficult to do; it takes effort and focused attention.

The Conscious and Unconscious Minds

Each one of us has two separate cognitive thinking systems: the conscious and the unconscious minds.

The conscious mind can be defined as the part of the mind where there are facts or feelings of which you are fully aware. For example, there is a tree outside my window and my eyes are blue. This is the part of the mind where all change takes place. We cannot change anything we are unaware of, so being aware is the first non-negotiable, necessary step to change.

The unconscious mind is the part of the mind which is inaccessible to the conscious mind, housing all of our deeply held beliefs and assumptions that consistently play in the background of our minds.

You're likely familiar with unconscious eating, like where you crush a bag of chips in one sitting while watching your favorite show. It's unconscious because you're not satiating a true hunger in your body with food that will provide you with sustained energy. You're likely feeding sadness, loneliness, disappointment, grief, or even simple boredom. That choice was made and carried out unconsciously.

Our unconscious minds are where all of our feelings and emotions reside, such as fear, sadness, disappointment, doubt, worry, anger, desire, love, and joy. Just because we're not aware or conscious of those feelings, does not mean they're not present. And just because we're not aware of them or we're ignoring them doesn't mean they're not impacting our experience.

Make no mistake: It is our unconscious mind that is driving the bus of our lives (picking up that bag of chips) and our relationships (shutting down to our partners).

The Upside and Downside of Efficiency

It is our brain's job to think; we can't stop it. It creates thoughts all day long – much of which is occurring through unconscious programming.

Our brains like to be efficient. Much like a computer, it is most efficient when it is performing the same activity time and time and time again.

Think about when you learned to drive a car. At first you had to consciously go through the steps in your mind to make sure nothing was missed.

Open the door.

Sit in the seat.

Put on seatbelt.

Put the key into the ignition.

Step on the brake and push or turn the key.

Adjust the mirrors.

Put the car into reverse.

Look in camera or over shoulder.

Take foot off brake and only step on gas if necessary.

Turn wheel.

Watch behind you.

Move car from reverse to drive.

Step on gas pedal.

Look in all your mirrors.

Now, you don't have to think about all of that. You grab your keys and the next thing you know you're on the freeway headed toward your destination. You do it unconsciously now because your brain has learned the steps.

This is what's absolutely miraculous about the pre-frontal cortex of the brain and how it learns. It learns the steps. It learns how to be efficient by learning the shortest path from point A to point B. It memorizes the steps and perfects them so that it becomes a skill. Once a skill is learned (driving a car, brushing your teeth, reading a book), your brain doesn't have to expend too much energy to accomplish the task.

Our brains make us incredibly efficient in our lives. That's the brain's job and it does it beautifully most of the time. Unless, of course, we're attempting to create change in our lives and our relationships.

Change isn't efficient. Your brain wants you to do the things the same way you've always done them – because that's what's efficient. But if you keep doing the same thing, you – for certain – will get the same result.

You know this intellectually. So if you're going to create change in your life and in your relationship, you will have to do what's completely inefficient: learn something new and do things differently than you've always done.

A Belief Is Just a Thought You Keep Thinking

I have many teachers, and one of the greatest teachers of my life is Abraham-Hicks, who taught me that a belief is just a thought you keep thinking. If you think the same thought over and over again, it won't take long for your brain to learn that thought and make it into a belief so that you don't have to continue to process it consciously. And once it becomes a belief, it just runs in the background of your mind, influencing your choices, actions, and behaviors unconsciously.

For instance, growing up, I learned that you don't talk about things that are ugly in your life.

You don't talk about your fears, your failures, or your insecurities. You don't talk about the big, hard curveballs that life throws at you, and the mistakes we all make in the process. You don't talk about the ugly that life can bring and the ugly emotions that appear. And when we have to hide those pieces of ourselves, all we're left with is a big pile of shame (that we also need to hide).

There was no one single event or single person that taught me this. It was just more of an underlying current that ran through our family, like an unwritten rule. And if you had to talk about the ugly, you certainly didn't do it publicly. (You can imagine how my family feels about the eight books I've written.)

I mentioned in the introduction that my grandfather struggled in his relationships, marrying many times after losing his wife. My grandmother – the love of my grandfather's life – died in a car accident where he was the driver. Surely there was a part of him that blamed himself, but he never showed that soft underbelly. He was an ex-Marine and was far more likely to show anger and blame than sadness and despair. My grandmother died when my mother was pregnant with me, so I never met her personally or saw the two of them together outside of photographs. I loved my grandpa, but I used to refer to him as "a hard man to love," because he was consistently cranky, judgmental, and critical. He wasn't the type of person anyone wanted to be with for long periods of time.

As a family, we never talked about the real cause of my grandmother's death. We never talked about why my grandpa was both sad and hateful at the same time. We never talked about his pain, but we certainly blamed him for his painful words and actions. We never talked about why my brother always acted out or why I always felt the need to overcompensate and be the good girl. We didn't discuss what it felt like when my father was forced to abandon his dream of being a pilot or my mother was told women can't be journalists. We didn't talk about why people with a different skin color were being shot by police or why priests who we were supposed to trust were sexually molesting innocent children. We didn't talk about why my mom would cry sometimes. We wouldn't dare talk about questions I had about the Catholic faith growing up or why my mother's father was an atheist. (If that's what he was. I'm not even sure because he never came to church with us and we never talked about it.) My brother didn't even tell me he was going to be a father until after my niece was born, because he held so much shame for having a child out of wedlock. And now that my sweet mother has Alzheimer's, we're supposed to avoid speaking about that elephant in the room as well.

I learned to say, "I'm good" and put on a happy face even if I wasn't. I subscribed to the "suck it up" philosophy and just kept moving forward. It's interesting, because before I knew about how the mind works, I just went along with what I had been taught. I never questioned it because I didn't know it should be or could be any different. I knew that when bad things happened, I was to pretend that everything was fine, even when it was far from fine. That was essentially the story of my entire first marriage. Make it look pretty on the outside (husband, home, cars, vacations, executive positions), even when it felt empty and alone inside.

Now that I know to question whether or not my unconscious programming actually serves me, I can no longer blame my family for anything. Now, if I choose to keep the belief that everything needs to look good even if it's not, that's on me. I'm no longer the victim of my upbringing by people that were only doing the best they could with what they had been taught themselves. This knowledge gives you choice. It gives you responsibility to yourself. It gives you power in your own life.

I could question the belief that *if it's ugly don't talk about it; put on a mask and just make it look good.* And when I looked closely at that belief system and saw how it was keeping me hidden, small, and frankly very lonely, I was able to change it and do so with compassion. I don't have to make anyone else wrong. I don't have the change the entire family and how they choose to live and breathe in their own lives. No one has to be wrong or ridiculed. But I do have to live and breathe what is true for me and do so as an aware, emotionally-mature woman who takes responsibility for my choices.

The only way we can ever change our unconscious beliefs is to bring them into the conscious and question them. Only then can we make some intentional choices about whether or not we want to keep that programming and whether or not it's helping us create the kind of life and relationships we desire.

The Lens

Imagine each one of us – everyone on this planet – is wearing a pair of eyeglasses. Embedded in the lenses are all these thousands of beliefs, created by millions of thoughts, shaped by billions of inputs and experiences all unique to us. And because no two people on the planet have had the exact same experiences in life and interpreted those experiences in the exact same way, no two people on the planet have the exact same lens through which they see and experience the world around them. Therefore, no one can truly understand our perspective, nor can we truly understand the unique view of others.

This plays out in our relationships every single day, in the simplest of ways and the most complicated of ways. One of my clients hadn't had sex with her husband in more than two years. Her husband was fine with it because through his lens he thought: "This is just how marriage is after being together for nineteen years and raising a family together. I love her and that should be enough." She, however, was devastated because she desired sex with her husband and felt rejected and alone after nearly two decades together. The situation is the same: No sex in the last two years. One is suffering and the other is not all as a result of the lens through which they see and interpret the situation.

Our unconscious minds are all about feeling. Our conscious minds are all about thinking. The bridge between the conscious and the unconscious are our belief systems. If we never look at them or question them, they remain hidden in the background, silently impacting every choice, action, and behavior. When we're willing to question our beliefs, we can then make conscious choices about whether or not that belief is serving us and whether or not we should keep it.

Here are some beliefs we've all been taught in some way through society, culture, family, expectations of other people, religion, and even children's movies:

There's a prince charming that will one day come along and save us.

We should grow up, get married, and have children.

Desire is bad.

It's selfish to put our needs in front of others' needs.

You should not question authority; just do as they tell you to do.

When you please others by meeting their needs, they will be loving towards you.

Good grades make you smart.

You should be successful (and everyone has their own opinion of what that looks like and how to get there).

For most of us, we never stop and question any of our beliefs. The brain's not going to do it, that's not efficient. We never look at our beliefs and explore whether they're helping us or hurting us. And we certainly don't seek reasons to consciously challenge or change them. The reason why is because we believe these thoughts and beliefs as Truths (with a capital T). By definition, no one intentionally believes something that they also hold as untrue or false. No one is walking around thinking, "Everything I think is probably a lie." So we believe these thoughts as Truth – and therefore draw the conclusion that anyone who does not hold the same beliefs is somehow wrong.

What Is Truth?

Have you ever heard the parable of the three blind men who come into a room with an elephant? One places his hand on the elephant's trunk, one places his hand on the side of the elephant, and the other, its tail. The man who is holding the elephant's trunk believes he's holding a snake. The man who is touching the side of the elephant believes he's touching a wall. And the man who is holding the elephant's tail believes he's holding onto a rope. Their beliefs about what each of them was touching was based upon their experience and interpretation of reality – not reality itself.

And it is the same with our beliefs.

Our beliefs are based on our interpretation of our experiences (and our family's interpretation, and our school's interpretation, and our religion's interpretation, etc.). When it comes down to what is actually true, almost everything is simply an interpretation that we believe.

What I know for certain is that you will never find another person on the planet who carries all the exact same interpretations as you – including (and maybe, especially) your spouse. So, maybe we can let our husbands off the hook a little bit when something is so painfully clear to us, but they don't see it at all. Their lens, their interpretations, and their beliefs are unique to them, just as yours are to you. And neither one of you have to be wrong, because it's simply a perspective.

Did You Know You Have a Pet Lizard?

You know that the pre-frontal cortex of the brain is where all the learning and reasoning happens. The lowest part of the brain is called the brain stem, or what scientists call the reptilian brain. They call it the reptilian brain because it is the oldest and most primitive part of the brain, but it's far from the most evolved part of the brain. My mentor, Martha Beck, refers to this as the lizard brain, mostly because it's more fun than referring to the reptilian brain, but also because it's so descriptive. The lizard brain is that part of us that if you don't watch it carefully and put some guard rails up, it will run away quickly and you won't be able to catch it. I call that the need to "keep your lizard on a leash."

The lizard part of your brain is where the fight or flight mechanism lives. It's the part of your brain that is responsible for keeping you safe and alive. That's its job. I so appreciate that effort.

Safe? Check.

Alive? Check.

Happy? Totally and completely irrelevant to the lizard brain.

The lizard brain is not responsible for helping you make decisions that will make you feel happy. To the contrary, it wants to keep you safe, which is many times the opposite of happy.

Opening your heart and falling in love can get you hurt: *Let's not do that.*

Trusting again after your blind trust has been broken: *That's dangerous.*

Making yourself vulnerable to your husband: *What if he rejects you? That would be humiliating and degrading.*

To keep you safe, your lizard brain is going to send you fearful messages all day long so that you don't do anything too scary. It's the part of our brains that love the idea of staying in your pajamas all day binge-watching reality shows of other people's lives. That's safe.

Do nothing and risk nothing. That way you'll never fail.

Stay small and stay invisible. You'll never be judged or rejected.

Do the same thing you did yesterday. It kept you alive and kept everyone around you more comfortable.

This is actually how people will remain stuck in indecision about their marriages – not staying and attempting to reconnect with their partners, but not leaving the marriages either. When you remain stuck in indecision, you never actually have to take any scary action one way or the other, so it serves you to remain stuck.

Stuck feels safe. It doesn't feel happy or comfortable, but to your lizard mind, at least it's safe here in the land of indecision.

Our lizard minds (when they're not kept on a leash) can take us to some dark places very quickly. Maybe the thoughts below sound familiar:

He'll never change.

This is all there is.

If I leave, what will people think?

I'll be judged.

I'll lose friendships...and people I love.

Where will I live?

Will I have enough money? Will I be able to do it on my own?

What if I never meet anyone and I'm alone forever?

Maybe this is better than being alone.

What will this do to my kids? I don't want to hurt my kids or disrupt their lives.

I won't have my kids all the time. I will have to share them and I'll feel so lost without them.

If we don't keep that lizard on a leash, our minds will very quickly have us living under a bridge with no health insurance, all alone, and ignored by our kids. None of that is actually true, nor has it likely ever been true. But it feels like it could be true and that will scare us into remaining paralyzed and not taking steps in any direction. So we never try to make the relationship better, but we never leave either.

If we don't realize what's really happening, then we're allowing these fearful thoughts running through our minds to direct our decisions (i.e., drive the bus). And usually that decision is some version of stay put and don't do anything!

Once you realize that those fearful thoughts are just that, thoughts, and that you get to choose whether or not to indulge them, you begin to feel more authority over your own life. Once you realize that everything you think isn't really Truth (with a capital T) and that you get to choose what you want to think and believe, you become very powerful in your own life. You actually get behind the wheel of your own bus so you can go to the places you want to go.

STEP TWO:
MANAGING THE MIND

"Between stimulus and response there is a space.
In that space is our power to choose our response.
In our response lives our growth and our freedom."
– Victor Frankl

Because it's trying to keep you safe, your lizard brain would prefer that you don't try to improve your marriage, that you don't reach for more, that you don't give life to the desires in your heart that have been whispering to you for a long, long time.

After all, if you don't try, then you won't ever fail.

And if you never fail, then you'll never feel the shame or negative emotion associated with failing.

Not even trying is what we in the coaching world call failing in advance. But failing in advance is still a form of failing. I would argue that it's worse than trying and not getting the result you desire, because then at least you know you tried and did your best.

We do all of this just to avoid the emotions we would feel if we tried to make our marriage feel good again and it didn't work. Seems silly, right?

What Are You Making This Mean?

One of my favorite questions to ask my clients is, "What are you making this mean?" Our minds give meaning to everything. Everything we experience goes through our lens and we give it meaning.

One person can try and not meet their goal and convince themselves that they're a failure and it will never work...at least not for them.

Whereas another person can try and not meet their goal and convince themselves that they're pretty badass just for trying. They might even think to themselves (as Einstein did), *I just learned one new way that won't work to help me reach my goal which means I'm that much closer to finding the answer.*

Albert Einstein often said, "Failure is success in progress." He made the conscious choice to view

his "failures" as simply learning what didn't work so that he could eventually find what did work.

We get to choose what we make failure mean for ourselves. We should choose consciously. We should choose wisely. When we don't consciously choose and we listen to our lizard minds, indulging all the fears and running from negative emotions, we'll never create anything great.

We'll never create the much needed change in our marriages.

We'll never get our own needs met.

We'll never feel good in the relationship.

The Model

I have many teachers. One of them is Master Life Coach Instructor at The Life Coach School, Brooke Castillo. She put structure around all the reasons why our thoughts and feelings are so important by creating what she calls The Model. She didn't create how this all works (the Universe did that), but she created a brilliant framework that makes it understandable, approachable, and relevant.

I'm going to walk you through each piece of The Model and then I'm going to help you use this inside of your struggling marriage. This is going to bring many pieces of the puzzle together for you in a meaningful way. If you get nothing else from this book and you snub your nose at all the other tools I'm providing, but you understand and begin to apply The Model in your life, it will be enough to completely transform your marriage. Don't skim by this. Be willing to dive in and really apply it.

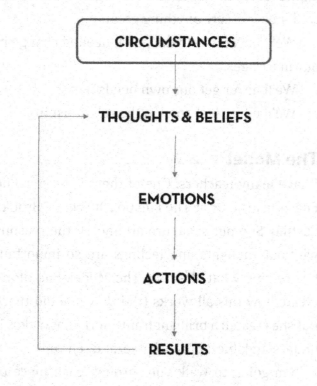

Brooke Castillo, The Self-Coaching Model

Circumstances

Circumstances are conditions in our lives. Some conditions are things we want in our lives. Some circumstances are things we do not want in our lives. Circumstances are neither positive nor negative. They're neutral. They're facts. They can be proven in a court of law. Here are some examples:

The wall is yellow.

I've been married twenty years.

My husband had an affair.

Yes, that's right. Even someone having an affair is not automatically negative. It is only a circumstance and therefore, it is neutral until we create a thought about it. Even though you could ask 100 people and get 99 of those to agree with you that this is a bad thing, it is still only a circumstance and therefore, neutral.

Many circumstances in our lives are within our control. Some are outside of our control. We can choose what color we paint the wall. We may be able to choose how long we remain married (although our spouses also have a say in that). We likely would never choose for our husbands to have an affair.

The circumstances only become positive or negative once we have a thought about that circumstance:

Yellow is a horrible color for a wall.

Staying together for twenty years is really a great accomplishment.

My husband shouldn't have had an affair.

These are thoughts. They are personal opinions and perspectives created through the lens of the person experiencing the circumstance. They are not facts.

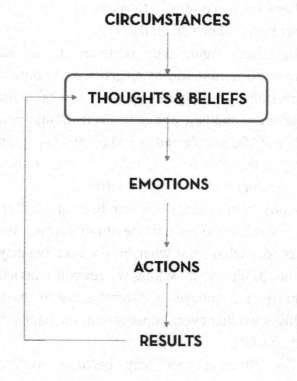

Brooke Castillo, The Self-Coaching Model

Thoughts

Our thoughts give context to our circumstances. It is said that the average human being has approximately 60,000 thoughts each day. Those of us with busy minds probably have many more. Because our mind likes to be efficient, much like a computer, it prefers to think the same thoughts over and over again. It's efficient to do the same thing repeatedly. It's inefficient to make the effort to think a new thought. And when we think the same thought repeatedly, it becomes a deeply held belief and those beliefs are embedded in our lenses.

Most of us believe our thoughts as though they are facts. We've never been taught to question our thoughts, so most of the world truly believes what's going on between their ears as irrefutable truths.

One person can look at the circumstance of the yellow wall and think it's pretty, while someone else thinks it's a tragic DIY project gone horribly wrong; same circumstance, different thought about that circumstance. Neither is right or wrong, they simply have different thoughts or a different perspective about a circumstance.

This same theory also applies to the circumstance of the husband who had an affair. Just because the majority of people think that statement is true doesn't make it a fact. It only makes it a perspective that many people agree upon. And many of us agree with that particular statement because we've all had similar conditioning about what is right and what is wrong. (I'm not encouraging affairs, by the way, I just like to use examples that will really highlight the teaching.)

Imagine how all of our relationships could shift with this one teaching alone: circumstances are neutral, and it is our thoughts about that circumstance that make it positive or negative. Our thoughts are not automatically true or "right," but rather just an opinion or our own personal perspectives. Imagine how the world would be a different place if we started to acknowledge the neutrality of circumstances and how everyone gets to create their own thoughts about those circumstances.

Let's use the most obvious, polarizing example possible to make the point. As I write this, Donald Trump is the president of the United States. Many people think he is incompetent, arrogant, and narcissistic. They think he's the worst president we've ever had in the history of our country. While still others (most of my family, frankly) have the perspective that he's strong, determined, and a great leader. They think he's exactly what the country needs most right now.

Who's right?

What if neither are right? What if neither are wrong?

What if everyone got to have their own thoughts and we didn't have to agree?

Imagine what this one teaching alone could do to your marriage. You and your partner can have different perspectives regarding the same circumstance and neither of you have to be wrong. You don't have to agree, but what you do need is have respect for one another's perspectives, without needing it to be the same as your own. When you stop trying to be right, you're not actively trying to make your partner wrong. From that place there's freedom, love, and respect inside the relationship that didn't exist before when you believed your thoughts as absolute, unequivocal truth.

And the best news of all is that no one can think for you and no one can force you to think or believe anything you don't want to think or believe. You get to create your own thoughts, your own perspectives. You do. So does your husband. Don't fight it. That's like arguing with reality and you will always lose that argument – 100% of the time. Embrace it. Become conscious about it. You get to choose how you want to think about any circumstance. For emphasis, I'll say that again: You get to choose how you want to think about any circumstance. Just think about how powerful that is. Now let everyone else off the hook from needing to have the same perspective.

Let's keep going...

CIRCUMSTANCES

↓

THOUGHTS & BELIEFS

↓

EMOTIONS

↓

ACTIONS

↓

RESULTS

Brooke Castillo, The Self-Coaching Model

Emotions

The thoughts we think are what create emotion within each of us. To show this, here's an experiment you can do:

Answer this question: What is the worst possible scenario that could happen if you don't fix the problems you're experiencing in your marriage? Describe that scenario here in detail:

_____

_____

_____

_____

As you think through this worst-case scenario, name one emotion that you're feeling:

_____

(Hint: worry, doubt, disappointment, despair, hopelessness...)

Take a few deep breaths in and out. You just held some negative energy in your body for a few minutes, so breathing deeply is the quickest way to release it.

Now, answer this question: What if everything you wanted to feel and experience in your marriage was not only possible, but probable? What would that look like or feel like? Describe it here in detail:

_____

_____

_____

_____

_____

_____

_____

_____

_____

_____

_____

_____

_____

_____

_____

_____

_____

_____

_____

_____

_____

_____

_____

Imagine that all of the dreams and desires you have for your marriage have now come true. Name at least one emotion that describes how you feel: _____.

(Hint: peaceful, grateful, hopeful, empowered, happy...)

By doing these exercises, you can very clearly see that the feelings (and maybe even physical sensations you felt) that were evoked within you were very different from one another.

Our thoughts create the emotions we're feeling.

Most people feel negative emotions when things are going badly in their lives and positive emotions when things are going well. They don't think there's any other option. This is why control-freaks attempt to control the conditions, circumstances, and people around them – they want to feel better and that's the only way they know how to do so.

We think the circumstances create our emotions, but that's not true. Our circumstances are neutral. It is our thoughts about those circumstances that create our emotions.

When you know that your thoughts are creating your emotions, and you realize you get to choose your thoughts, now all of a sudden you have a lot more control about how you feel as you move through your life.

Why Emotions Are Important

If you're like most people, you are probably tempted to skip this part as most of us do our best to avoid emotions at all costs.

As women, we are told, "Oh don't be so emotional." Young girls were shamed for expressing emotion because it made others uncomfortable. Those young girls grow up to be women who are told that their emotions make them irrational and therefore, not good leaders – reinforcing the belief that emotions need to be suppressed at all costs.

The men in our lives were taught from a very young age that big boys don't show emotion and that doing so makes them less of a man. They inevitably heard things like "Boys don't cry," and "Suck it up, be a man," or "Toughen up." Expressing emotions such as sadness, fear, or insecurity will get you a one way ticket to a testosterone drenched beat-down in the locker room. Boys who learn not to express much emotion grow up to be men who do not express emotion. And then we wonder why we find it difficult to connect with the men in our lives.

It is for all these reasons that we don't have great language or tools around emotions. This is actually an enormous problem. Because it is emotions that are in the driver's seats of our lives – whether we are aware of it or not.

This is what's happening when we say angry, hurtful things to people we love that we wish we could take back. This is what's happening when we respond with sarcasm because we're afraid of being vulnerable and really expressing what's in our hearts. This is what's happening when we know we should have protected someone being mistreated, but we were too scared.

Our emotions are driving our actions.

And of course, it is our actions that will determine the results we each experience in our lives.

So if we don't like the results we have in our marriages, we have to become much more conscious about managing our thoughts so that we can experience more positive emotions and start taking actions that align with who we want to show up as in our lives.

That, my friends, is how you will create change in your most important, most intimate relationship. If that's not apparent to you, go back and reread it again and again until it is apparent. This is the answer you've been looking for.

Applying the Model

You'll recall that learning something new is important, but we cannot stop there. If we do, we just become a little bit smarter. It is only when we begin applying what it is we've learned that we create real change in our lives.

Here are some examples from some of my clients:

Debbie and Nick had been together for twelve years. They had three boys ages 7-11. He had a successful accounting practice and she was a full-time nurse practitioner. Like many couples, they struggled to make themselves and their relationship a priority. They placed their focus and their energy into their kids and their careers, keeping the home running and the bills paid. Nick seemed to be okay with that because by the time he got home in the evenings, he was exhausted. But Debbie wanted more. She wanted a connection again with Nick. She wanted to feel loved and desired again. She would tell Nick she wanted to spend more time together, but he would never plan anything for them and he often prioritized family above their relationship as a couple. She feared that things would never change and over time grew more and more resentful toward him. When she reached out to me, she was very seriously considering divorce and had she created a model it would have looked much like this:

Circumstance: The only time Nick and Debbie spend time together is as a family with the kids, and with their busy lives, they're both exhausted at the end of the day with nothing left to give to each other.

Thought: He doesn't want to try. He doesn't care. Everything seems to get prioritized over her, even his business and workouts. She doesn't want to argue with him and she doesn't want to have to beg for his love either.

Emotion: sadness, despair, worry, doubt, defeat

Action: Debbie shuts down from Nick. She stops expressing her needs and begins doing more with friends.

Result: The distance between Debbie and Nick widens and the resentments increase. Debbie begins to give up hope and stops trying, stops reaching for change. She begins to think about what life would be like with someone else. Maybe the grass can be greener. She thinks leaving may be the only option.

This is a slippery slope to an affair or eventual divorce.

When most people want to change the result, they start attempting to control the actions – telling their husbands what they need them to do differently and expecting him to take those actions. But spouses don't take action because someone else tells them to. Action is driven from emotion. Action is taken from desire within themselves or a lack of action is taken from a place of confusion.

A confused mind does nothing. When we don't know what to do, often we take no action. That is very often the common response from husbands when wives start to ask for more in the marriage. This is a broad generalization, so certainly it is not universally true. But men tend to be goal-oriented and women tend to be better at nurturing. From a man's perspective, the day you said, "I do," the goal was achieved and he moved onto the next goal, which may have been a new home, making more money, or excelling in his career. Because women are natural nurturers, it is often women who are nurturing the relationship. We have lots of ideas about how we could become closer as a couple and we cannot understand why our husbands don't also have ideas, or more importantly, a desire to take those actions.

It's not a lack of love. It's a lack of desire. It's a lack of motivation. It's a lack of payoff.

This is why, unfortunately, it is often after one spouse makes the decision that they're done that all of a sudden there's a desire on their partner's part to make the necessary changes and prioritize the relationship in a way they hadn't previously. Crisis always ignites motivation and desire.

If Debbie's husband felt the same desire to improve the marriage and knew what actions to take in order to achieve that goal, he would have done it. And because the thoughts, he doesn't want to try...he doesn't care...I'm his last priority... were present for Debbie, she was pretty skeptical and not exactly open to and appreciative of any efforts he was attempting to make.

I worked with Debbie for eight weeks. She began applying all the same tools I'm sharing with you in this book and through our work together, she was able to change the results she was experiencing in her marriage by changing her thoughts about the circumstances. The circumstance did not change. Her thoughts about that circumstance changed and that changed everything. Here's what that looked like:

Circumstance: The only time Nick and I spend together is as a family with the kids and with our busy lives, we're both exhausted at the end of the day with nothing left to give to each other.

Thought: We've both been placing a priority on our careers and the kids. If we prioritize the relationship above the kids and our careers, our kids will be happier and more secure seeing their mom and dad be more loving toward one another, and we'll be more inspired and more productive in our jobs (likely getting more done in less time).

Emotion: hopeful, excited, empowered

Action: Debbie started to make her relationship a priority. (Rather than complaining about all that she wanted Nick to do, she began giving to him what she wanted for herself.) She began to send loving, affectionate texts to him during the day. She would plan activities for the two of them to do together. She even made physical advances toward Nick.

Result: They were spending more time together. They were talking and sharing their hearts more. They had become closer. Because he felt confident and loved, he started to follow her lead and took more action himself toward making the marriage a priority.

For the Skeptics

All too often, when people hear about changing their thoughts, they immediately think they need to lie to themselves and settle for not getting their needs met. That's not what this is. It's worth saying again. *Lying to yourself is NOT what I'm asking you to do.*

Whatever thought you change, it still has to feel just as true as the original thought. Debbie believed that if she and Nick became a priority, then her boys would benefit from that and so would her career. She believed that new thought just as much as her original thought that Nick didn't care, he didn't want to try, and that she wasn't a priority.

The thoughts you change have to be equally true. The reason we can always identify a different thought that will feel better and get us closer to our desired result is because there are always many truths to every circumstance. There is never only one way to see a circumstance.

Later, I'll discuss more about how to bridge thoughts, but for now, just begin to play with The

Model, looking for opportunities to apply it. You can enter into The Model anywhere. You can begin with a circumstance just as easily as you can start with an emotion you're feeling and backing into the thought that's causing that emotion. You can apply The Model to thoughts about your marriage just as readily as you can apply it to rainy day weather. The only way to become truly adept at using this tool is through repetition.

***

Challenge: Write down at least one application of The Model each day for the next two weeks. You only get better at what you practice, so if you want to be able to shift your thoughts in a moment, this needs to become second-nature.

***

Not Every Thought Has to Be Changed

If we have 60,000+ thoughts every day and all of them need to be changed, we'd be in trouble. We don't have to analyze every single thought we have and go through the work of changing those thoughts. Instead, we just have to pay attention to the thoughts that do not pass through these two gates:

- Does it feel good when I think that thought?
- Am I getting the results I desire?

If either of those is a "no," then it's time to dig a little deeper to change the thought. You can usually tell the thoughts that need some work by the way they feel. When you start to feel negative emotion (worry, doubt, anger, etc.), it's time to pay attention to get at the thought that's creating the negative emotion and work The Model all the way through.

Good News. Bad News.

You likely would agree with me that we are responsible for what we do, but we are also just as responsible for the thoughts we think. The thoughts we create drive all of our emotions and our emotions create our actions. And of course, the actions we take will create the results in our lives. When we're not happy with the results we're experiencing, it's time to manage the mind more deliberately and begin to think and feel on purpose.

It's good news and bad news, really: We have 100% control over what we think and what we think is what's creating our experience. We can choose to look at this as daunting or we can choose to see how powerful we truly are. Both those thoughts could be true, but they will create very different emotions and very different results.

I actually have more good news, bad news.

Now that you know this you can't un-know it. Now that you know how the mind works, you can't go back to believing every single thing you think as the absolute truth. You can no longer pretend that some people are naturally happy and others are not. Feeling happy on purpose takes effort. It's efficient for the brain to think doom-and-gloom in order to keep you safe and sound. That takes no effort, no creativity. That's probably why most people do it so frequently. It takes a bit of effort to force your mind to go looking for a truthful thought that feels better when you think it, but I promise the pay-off is worth the effort, because it will completely change the results you're experiencing in your life and your relationship.

STEP THREE: FINDING OPPORTUNITIES TO CREATE CHANGE

"As long as you think that the cause of your problem is 'out there'—as long as you think that anyone or anything is responsible for your suffering—the situation is hopeless. It means that you are forever in the role of victim, that you're suffering in paradise."

– Byron Katie

Bridging the Conscious and Unconscious

Dr. Bruce Lipton has said that the subconscious mind can process 20 million bits of information per second, but the conscious mind can only process 40 bits of info per second. That means the subconscious mind can process 500,000 times more than the conscious mind. That's a lot.

So what if the data we carry in our unconscious minds is what's getting in the way of creating the kind of loving and connected relationship we desire? Are we screwed? Not at all. Here's why:

The minute we are willing to identify those unconscious thoughts, beliefs, and judgements and bring them into our conscious awareness, we are able to make a decision about whether or not we want to keep them.

For instance, the brain will often look to the past to create a picture of what is possible for you in the future. This is why couples will automatically assume that *this is just how marriage is* after being together for decades. It's what they saw and experienced with their parents, it's what they see around them in other couples, and they don't know that anything else is possible because they've never seen it or experienced it themselves. The data our brains have gathered from the past would not help us determine that something new, something neither of you have ever seen or experienced before, is possible. When we stop there and don't question that belief, we remain stuck in the circumstance of that experience.

Every advancement in our society has required someone to look beyond what they've seen or experienced previously in order to create something new. Inventors, scientists, and innovators often see a problem and look for ways to solve that problem. Sometimes that's taking a current solution and improving upon it and sometimes that's creating something entirely new that hasn't existed previously.

You need look no further than your cell phone to drive the point of innovation home. Cell phones were initially created so that we could speak to people in those in-between times when we weren't at home or at work. They were originally marketed as a safety net should we need it, like in case our cars broke down on the side of the road. But now no one even wants to use the phone for talking to other people. Instead, most people prefer to use it as a mobile computer, a camera, a video recorder, as voice recorder, and a music library. From our phones, we can order pizza just as easily as we can order a car to pick us up at our doorstep – all without ever speaking to another human being. There was nothing in our past that would have shown us that was possible.

If we only ever looked to our past to show us what is possible for the future, not a single person would be walking around with a cell phone today. And yet, almost every person, in virtually every country, at every income level has a cell phone today.

You've got to start applying that same mental philosophy to the thoughts about what is possible for your life and marriage. Just because you've never seen it in other people's relationships, nor have you experienced it yourself, does not mean that a loving, connected, committed relationship is not possible, even after you've been together for decades. If you want something others don't have, you have to be willing to do things that others have not done. You have to be willing to challenge the thoughts and beliefs sitting in your unconscious by bringing them into your conscious. Then consciously (pun intended) change those thoughts to something that gets you closer to the outcome you desire.

We cannot change anything we're not aware of, so in order to create change, we have to recognize it. To unwind the unconscious programming, we need to bring it into our conscious awareness and one of the places to begin is by looking at the recurring patterns that play out over and over again in our lives.

Interrupting Patterns

Unlike counseling and therapy which tend to look at your childhood and history, coaching focuses on your present and where it is you want to go. While looking at your history absolutely helps you understand how you got to this place in your relationship, it does very little with helping you move forward, unless you want to continue to create more of the same. There's a reason why the windshield in your car is huge and the rearview mirror is small. It's far more important to be able to see where you're headed than where it is you've been.

All that being said, you and your partner have a pattern of engagement around the issues in your marriage and if we can identify the details of that pattern, then we can make some conscious choices about how to interrupt that pattern in order to create a different result.

A client of mine that I will refer to as Daniela had been married to her husband, Cole, for eighteen years. They had two children together, now seventeen and fifteen years old. Daniela had always been fiercely independent, having a successful career as an entrepreneur, while Cole had been the more steady, safe, and reliable. The couple had experienced their fair share of heartbreak, with eight miscarriages and a mother passing of breast cancer. Cole's way of dealing with life's difficult situations was to not talk about it; his likely thinking was *if we don't talk about it then it never really happened*. Daniela needed to talk about these things and many more, and not being able to do so with Cole left her feeling isolated and alone.

Occasionally, when she was bothered or hurt by something Cole did or didn't do, she would attempt to talk to him about it. She would express how she felt and her feelings would be quickly invalidated by Cole. That led to arguments, each trying to be heard by the other, and defending their position until someone walked away in anger and they gave one another the silent treatment for a few days. But Daniela never was heard, Cole felt attacked, and nothing was ever resolved. This pattern happened over and over again and because nothing was ever truly resolved, small resentments mounted over time that created distance and animosity in the relationship. Here's what it looks like:

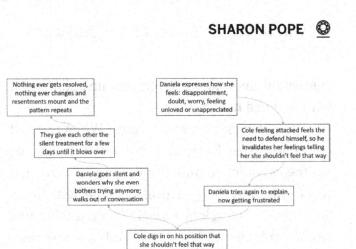

Nothing ever gets resolved, nothing ever changes and resentments mount and the pattern repeats

Daniela expresses how she feels: disappointment, doubt, worry, feeling unloved or unappreciated

They give each other the silent treatment for a few days until it blows over

Cole feeling attacked feels the need to defend himself, so he invalidates her feelings telling her she shouldn't feel that way

Daniela goes silent and wonders why she even bothers trying anymore; walks out of conversation

Daniela tries again to explain, now getting frustrated

Cole digs in on his position that she shouldn't feel that way

Where Daniela has remained stuck is in the pattern that her husband should understand how she feels and want to talk about it and because he clearly doesn't, he's wrong. Cole, not wanting to be wrong, has remained stuck in the same painful pattern that he needs to defend his position and make her wrong in order to avoid talking about problems. Both, in their desire to be heard, to be validated, and ultimately to be right, are digging themselves further and further into a hole as a couple.

When Daniela and I mapped this out, she was then able to make some conscious choices about where she could do it differently and interrupt the pattern of engagement with Cole. The first place she went was to change the way in which she began expressing how she felt. Rather than stating her feelings as an accusation or criticism, she would own how she felt and just share that with him in a neutral way.

The conversation went from, "When you left me alone when I was sick last week, you made me feel abandoned and unloved," to "I know that when you're sick, you prefer to be left alone. So, when I was sick last week, you did what you would probably want me to do and gave me space to rest. But I thought it would be important for you to know that when I'm sick, I really need you near me because I'm going to feel more sad and anxious during those times. Here's what that can look like...."

Because it wasn't wrapped in the envelope of an accusation to something Cole was doing wrong, he was better able to hear what she was expressing. Plus, she had identified that she had never really told Cole what she needed. She assumed that he should know what she needed. When her needs weren't being met, she got quietly angry and cold toward him, assuming he would interpret this passive-aggressive behavior as something he should do differently and therefore make the necessary changes. I don't have to tell you that's not what happened.

Diane Sawyer once said, "A criticism is just a really bad way of making a request...so just make the request."

Now she was able to express what she needed and Cole was able to hear her. The arguments became fewer and the resentments about not feeling heard began to dissipate within Daniela.

Apply It:

Write down the pattern of engagement that you have with your spouse around the issues in your marriage. It's always circular in nature and oftentimes there's no resolution. Write down each of the steps on a single sheet of paper looking something like this:

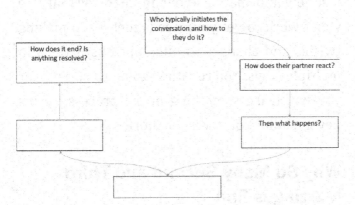

Identify one area where you're willing to do it differently in order to interrupt the pattern. That could be changing the way in which you say it, as Daniela did. It could be not walking away or not engaging in the silent treatment. It could be more questions, genuinely seeking to understand your partner's perspective before needing them to understand your perspective.

If you keep engaging in the same way, there's no reason to believe that anything will change and the problems will be resolved. But when you change just one piece in the pattern, it changes your partner's reactions and has downstream impacts to the rest of the pattern. Even if the first change doesn't work magically, as Daniela's did, you will gain some new information, even if it's just new information about another way that also won't work to get your needs met. Keep making tweaks and changes to interrupt this pattern in multiple ways. You're either going to succeed or you will learn something in the process, so it's never a failure or a wasted effort.

Why So Many Second and Third Marriages End

Research estimates that somewhere between 40%-50% of first marriages end in divorce. But the more staggering numbers are for subsequent marriages:

- 67% of second marriages end in divorce
- 74% of third marriages end in divorce

That's not a coincidence.

That's because most people think the problem within the relationship is the other person and never look back at their own role so that they can do it differently in the future.

Their minds tell them that, *If my husband is the issue, then as soon as I get rid of my husband, the issue is resolved.* But that's not the full truth, even if it is his behavior that is the problem in the relationship. You're in the relationship, so even if you displayed nothing but perfect and unconditional love toward your husband (tell the truth now...), there are some things that you did to foster the environment that has contributed to your experience.

- You overlooked or allowed bad behavior
- You didn't tell the truth about your needs or clearly articulate your boundaries
- You were not clear about who you were and what you deserved
- You accommodated his need to control you or the circumstances of your lives, teaching and enabling him to believe that his path to peace was through controlling you, your actions, and your behaviors
- You taught him that the way he was treating

you was okay, because you didn't want to stand up and say otherwise.

There is always, always some gold that can be mined from owning your part and taking responsibility for that in the creation of our experiences.

Here's the problem and the reason for such an incredibly high rate of second and third divorces: If we haven't yet taken personal responsibility for ourselves and our role in the creation of our own experience, we end up unintentionally re-creating similar dysfunction within the next relationship. Even if we leave the current relationship under the pretense that it was all his fault, we're taking ourselves with us. And whether we want to admit it or not, we helped create the dysfunction in the relationship. So it's a worthwhile effort to own it and clean it up, whether it's for the benefit of this relationship or another one in the future.

The other part of looking back that I think is relevant to your struggling and disconnected relationship is to take a second and consider what you learned at home from your family about what love and marriage looked like. Spending just ten minutes really considering what they demonstrated to you through their actions and interactions is plenty to help you understand your own actions, choices, and behaviors. No need to spend months here navel-gazing and dissecting every element of who your parents were and where they fell down in their parenting skills. They did the best they could with what they knew and the skills and tools they had available to them at the time. Plus, like all of us, they were carrying their own wounds and that played out in their lives and relationships. The generational fears and habits are typically painfully obvious and once you can see them (bringing them into your conscious awareness), you can make some decisions about whether or not you want to carry them forward and continue to have them impacting you.

There is some benefit from looking backward, but doing so definitely slows you down so you don't want to stay there long. If you look back with the intention of using historic information in order to create a new future, however, that small look over your shoulder can be helpful.

Get clear about how you played a role in the creation of your relationship experience – even if that's only what you allowed or overlooked.

Secondly, get clear about what your childhood experience taught you – and how it still influences you today – so you can make some conscious choices for yourself about its impact moving forward.

We cannot change anything we're unaware of, so awareness is enough here to create massive change. Most of this book – and all of my teachings – are focused around how to do relationships differently so that we can start to create more evolved relationships that work and feel good to both people. That's a forward focus, for sure. But there is some benefit in looking backward strategically to avoid making the same mistakes unconsciously time and again.

Forgiving Daily

No one really wants to forgive. Most of us want to hang onto the idea that we're right and therefore, justified in holding resentments toward those we claim to love. And, in doing so, we think that on some level that we're causing the person who hurt us to suffer somehow or that we're teaching them a lesson. But that's not how it works. Carrying unhealed resentments leaves us carrying the weight of those resentments through our lives, keeping us in our own self-imposed prisons and we're the only ones with the key.

Think of resentments as a 20 lb. weight that we carry around on our shoulders every day, all day. Even when we're not thinking about it or focused upon the hurt, we're carrying the weight of the hurt with us everywhere we go. No one has the ability to take that 20 lb. weight from us. We're the only ones that can make the choice to set it down. But it will stay there until we make the conscious choice to forgive others for the hurts they inflicted.

Just as carrying any judgements serves to separate us from one another, carrying resentments also serves to cause unnecessary separation between ourselves and our partners. That separation is an illusion, placing a hierarchy in the relationship that is not real or possible. According to A Course in Miracles, "Forgiveness is the healing of the perception of separation."

In our marriages, forgiveness needs to be at least as consistent as brushing our teeth. Sometimes it will be our beloveds that we need to forgive and sometimes it will be ourselves, but forgiving over and over and over again is the only real path to a truly loving relationship with one another.

I have a theory. I don't know for certain that it's true, but it brings me a great deal of peace in my life and dramatically improves all my relationships. The theory is that at any given time, with the tools we have available to us in that moment, we're all just doing the best we can.

You're doing the best you can. So is your partner.

Even when we let ourselves or one another down.

Even when we don't live up to our own or one another's expectations.

Even when we mess it up and it's not terribly graceful or elegant.

In that moment, that was our best.

Plenty of people have let me down in my life. (I'm not different from you in that regard, even though I try to not carry expectations of others.) But when I'm able to see their actions through the lens of this theory that we're all doing the best we can, I am able to find compassion rather than judgement – and that makes all the difference in how I feel in that moment and how I feel about them.

Compassion will always feel better than judgement.

Forgiveness will always feel better than resentment.

Love will always feel better than hate or anger or criticizing.

STEP FOUR:
THE COLD, HARD TRUTH

*"No matter how difficult and painful it may be,
nothing sounds as good to the soul as the truth."*
– Martha Beck

The Kiss of Death for Your Marriage

Occasionally, a marriage will blow up quickly and end as a result of one single incident such as infidelity. But, more often than not, it's the small, day-to-day hurtful words and actions between a couple that dissolve a marriage slowly over time. And almost nothing can chip away at a marriage more directly than one or both partners' need to be right when there's a disagreement.

The desire to be right is something that was taught to us at a very young age. When we got the answers right in school, we got better grades. Better grades meant better schools and more opportunities. We went out into competitive working environments and those that received the promotions seemed to be those that made the right choices and had the fewest failures.

But that which has made us successful in school and work can be the very thing that destroys our most important and most intimate relationships. We didn't consciously drag this same approach to solving problems into our marriages in an effort to make our partners wrong. It becomes an unconscious pattern of engagement that shows up occasionally. And it's the very thing that can undermine us from creating the kind of connected, loving marriage we want for ourselves.

Here's why the need to be right can be the kiss of death for a marriage:

We're Not Listening

When our desire is to be right, we're not listening to our partners. We may be dominating the conversation, talking over our partners, and not fostering an environment for healthy dialogue with the one we promised to love and cherish. We may be interrupting our partners or not actively listening

because we're thinking about the next rebuttal that will align with our beliefs and ideologies that will make us, at least in our own minds, right.

We Learn Nothing New

There's a quote by Pema Chödrön that says, "The truth you believe and cling to makes you unavailable to hear anything new." When we're so tied to our own views and opinions, we don't allow ourselves the opportunity to learn anything new. If we don't think our spouses have valid, interesting ideas and insights, then why did we choose them as our lifelong partners? It's been my experience that there is nothing and no one that can teach us more – mostly about ourselves – than our spouses. Our role is to remain open to the lesson in order to grow beyond that unconscious programming.

We Remain Stuck in the Past

When we're not learning anything new, the only insights from which we have to draw upon for making decisions is the past: our past experiences, our past failures, our past relationships (that obviously didn't work or we would still be there). And when we're focused on the past, we unintentionally perpetuate those same experiences, bringing them into the present and allowing them to impact the future. This is how we repeat the same relationship mistakes over and over again and experience repeated heartache inside the relationship.

There Is No Hierarchy in a Healthy Relationship.

If we behave as though our beloved's opinion isn't valuable, it can create an unintentional hierarchy within the relationship where one partner feels better than or smarter than the other. The best relationships are comprised of equals with mutual respect for one another, which cannot occur when we're not willing to listen to and consider one another's opinions to be just as valid as our own.

It Limits Our Ability to Connect

Prioritizing the need to be right in an important conversation with our spouses will limit our ability to connect with them. Through my coaching practice, the one thing I hear more than any other thing that's missing inside of a struggling marriage is connection between the partners. But when we have to be right, then the other person is automatically wrong. And when we feel like we're consistently being made to feel like we're wrong, that's not someone we're anxious to curl up next to at night.

The need to be right shows up in subtle ways. For instance, I had a client, Dawn, who had been married to Brad for thirty-four years. Dawn was fun and outgoing. Her kids were now grown and starting families of their own so she now wanted to get out and enjoy life. She had a wide circle of friends, loved to travel, and owned her own business. It seemed like she always had plans, and at least once a month she liked to go to the big casino in their city to play slot machines with her girlfriends.

Brad was more serious, an engineer by trade. He preferred to stay home, cook, and spend time with family or close friends. His idea of getting away was the comfortable beach house they had purchased years ago that was only a four-hour drive away. And Brad would get irritated when Dawn wanted to go to the casino. It always seemed to lead to an argument between them.

He felt strongly that it was a waste of time and money – a frivolous and unnecessary indulgence. Dawn saw it as entertainment, a fun evening out with friends and, to some degree, resented having to explain herself. They both felt they were right (and a little righteous). They would each argue to prove their point, backed up with both facts and feelings, attempting to get the other to see their perspective. They had this same argument dozens of times and each time it placed another wedge between them.

What if neither of them was right?

Recall how each of us has a lens through which we see and experience the world around us. Embedded in that lens are decades of thoughts, beliefs, judgements, experiences, and opinions. No two people on the planet have the exact same lens because no two people have had the exact same life experiences that led them to the exact same conclusions. So, although our own opinions seem painfully, obviously accurate and correct to us, it's unlikely that someone else – even your life partner – will see all the important parts of the relationship the exact same way.

This was absolutely the case with Dawn and Brad. They could not see one another's perspective – and frankly didn't want to. They had drastically different opinions about this topic and were convinced that their perspective was the right perspective.

Dawn wasn't wrong for wanting to do something that was fun for her and gave her a few hours of happiness with friends. And Brad wasn't wrong for not choosing to go to the casino and gamble, instead remaining closer to home.

Neither is wrong.

And truthfully, neither is right either.

They each have an opinion, a preference.

And because they couldn't (or wouldn't) see this as a simple difference in preferences, they had this same argument again...and again...and again.

You Don't Have to Have the Same Preferences

Some couples like to do the same things. Some don't.

My husband likes to fish; I do not.

Who's right? No one.

I don't wish he wouldn't fish or give him a hard time about going fishing. I don't shame him for not being more productive. I don't make it mean that he loves fishing more than he loves me (because if he loved me, wouldn't he rather spend time with me than the fish?).

You don't have to be carbon-copies of one another in order to make the relationship work, but you do have to respect the other person's preferences, not attempting to make them wrong and bend to your will.

If I placed a pillow over your face, what would you do? You would surely fight to get the pillow removed. When we attempt to control our partners' actions and behaviors, it will always feel like a pillow over the face and their natural reaction will be to fight back and defend themselves. In this case, they're defending their position. This is just basic human instinctual behavior.

And the nature of needing to be right is that you automatically make your partner wrong.

None of this lends itself to creating more closeness within the relationship.

Let him have his perspective. He doesn't need to agree with you or see your point in order for your own experience to be valid. You can even let him be downright wrong (in your not-so-humble opinion) and not make it mean anything about you.

Rather than expending so much effort into being right in our relationships, we could choose to spend much less effort and let our partners have their perspectives when we don't agree. When we're willing to do that, we help to create a relationship where both people feel safe, valued, heard, important, and equal. And having that kind

of a relationship is worth so much more than being right about one sticky issue.

Will the Real You Please Step Forward?

No one remains as the exact same person over the course of decades. We all change and evolve and grow...sometimes in the same direction as our partners and sometimes in different directions. And sometimes the person you thought you married isn't actually the person you married.

When Katie met Tony they had a lot in common. They both placed a priority on family, both were very driven in their respective professions, and both lived a very active lifestyle. The first few years of their marriage together Katie was running three businesses while Tony was an advertising executive, they were typically flipping at least one home at any given time, and they took plenty of ski trips together. They never had a great sex life, but it seemed like a fair trade-off at the time for Katie, since Tony absolutely adored her and they had fun together, genuinely enjoying one another's company.

Katie now refers to that version of Tony as The Representative.

The Representative liked to stay out late, talking, and drinking together until the wee hours of the morning, connecting, looking into one another's eyes.

The Representative liked careening down a mountain on skis or taking trips to the beach together.

The Representative liked being with friends and family. He was always the one down on the floor playing with his nieces and nephews at family functions.

The Representative worked hard and was proud of his work.

The Representative was fun. He was present. Katie knew she could make a life with The Representative.

And then after being married for ten years and having two children, The Representative was nowhere to be found, and she didn't know the person Tony was now. She was a smart woman, but had she been duped?

Now, Tony preferred a cold beer and a hammock on a Sunday afternoon, rather than a ski slope.

Now, Tony didn't really want to play with the kids or make sure they got on the bus okay in the morning.

Now, Tony didn't want to make plans with friends and family – and kind of resented when she wanted to do so.

Now, Tony took a lot of time off from work, lost his ambition, and ended up getting fired from his job.

Now, Katie was trying to figure out who it was she's married to and which Tony was the real version. For obvious reasons, she feared it was the latter version of Tony and she began questioning her marriage. She made the decision to leave, and all of a sudden, The Representative showed up again, attempting to be the fun guy and the engaged dad. It was very confusing.

Katie genuinely wanted to know who her husband really was, even if it was different from what she thought or what she wanted in a partner. He's the father of her children and she wanted to know the real Tony. He was afraid to show her that man for fear of losing her, but she felt lied to and deceived – even robbed of being able to fully know this man she had married.

We have got to be fully ourselves in relationships. That doesn't mean that we won't change, grow, or evolve, but all along the way, we've got to tell the truth about who we really are. When we're attempting to be who we think others want us to be so they will approve of us or love us, we're doing what I call The Hustle. We're hustling for approval, hustling for love, and hustling for acceptance. And hustling is essentially lying. We can do that dance for a few months or even a few years, but it is not sustainable for a lifetime.

Eventually, your partner will see the real you. Eventually the truth always shows up. If they're going to love you, you want them to love the real you, not some contrived version of you. The Representative isn't sustainable over the long haul of marriage.

Katie ultimately made the decision to leave the marriage with Tony, but she did so in the most loving way possible. Tony wasn't a bad guy or a villain, he just wasn't who she thought he was. She genuinely loved him, she just no longer wanted to be in an intimate relationship with him. And it was so peaceful because they realized they simply wanted different things and now they're doing an amazing job of co-parenting their young children, respecting one another, and moving forward in their lives knowing they did what was right for each of them. That doesn't mean it wasn't painful or that there weren't really emotional moments, but it does mean that they allowed each other to be who they really are, fully loving and accepting that person, and still making a difficult choice.

If You Would Only Be Different, Then You'd Be Perfect

My client Tammy was married to Nathan for twelve years when she reached out to me. Tammy was the kind of woman who really wanted to get out and live fully. She wanted deep relationships, meaningful experiences, and even as a working professional mother of three, she still wanted fun and excitement in her life. Nathan preferred being at home and being with family. His idea of getting out was to go to the gym, which he did regularly. He didn't need lots of excitement, instead preferring stability, consistency, and ease in his life.

They did have vastly different preferences, and yet, neither was right or wrong. They became locked in the recurring cycle of wanting the other to change. Tammy wanted Nathan to be more spontaneous and exciting, so that she could feel more alive. Nathan wanted Tammy to want to watch TV with him and sleep late on the weekends so that he could feel more at ease in his life.

One of my favorite sayings is from Abraham-Hicks: "If you would be different, I would feel better."

Virtually every single one of us does this to our partners in some way. We want them to be different so that we can feel some version of better (safe, alive, happy, better in some way). Typically, we want them to be like us because that's what would make us feel better.

We should be aligned on how we parent our children.

We should agree on the balance between spending and saving.

We should both want to get out and live life with the same level of excitement and adventure.

We should believe the same things and have the same priorities.

We should have the same level of libido and each want sex at a similar frequency level.

Wouldn't that be nice?

When all the stars align like that in a relationship consistently, it must feel lovely. I wouldn't know because I've never seen it or experienced it (and I've seen thousands of relationships).

We're not the same people, so why is our expectation that we should see things the same way? We were not born from the same gene pool. We did not have the same upbringing. We do not have the same scars and traumas. We do not have the same tastes and preferences. We do not have the same lens through which we see and experience the world.

But when we have that expectation, we jump into trying to change and control our partners so that we can feel better in some way. But what if you could feel better without him needing to change at all?

All you have to do is stop looking to him to be the portal through which you feel good as you move through your life. That is a choice that you could make today: feel however you want to feel about the circumstances of your life and manage your thoughts to create that feeling.

As long as you have the thought that he should be different, you will create emotions like irritation, upset, and even hopelessness. You wishing he would be different is the equivalent of asking an apple to turn into an orange. It doesn't happen, you get frustrated, and no one feels loved, accepted, or connected. Any time you argue with reality, you will be frustrated. The moment you change that thought to *he gets to be him and I get to be me*, you create emotions more like contentment, optimism, and peacefulness. No one has to be different for you to feel better when taking responsibility for how you feel.

Drop the Scorecard

One of the misunderstandings we carry into our marriages is that there is a finite amount of work to be done, and with two people in the relationship, that workload will be divided in half forever. We think, therefore, that life will become easier when we have a partner.

That seems perfectly logical, except that the amount of work we tend to add to our plates after we get married seems to increase substantially. We might have a home, or a bigger home than we had previously. We might have new interests that we want to do together as a couple. We might have children, and then the amount of work on our plates as a couple just shot through the roof. Typically the amount of things that need to be done when you're in a relationship is much more than what you had on your plate as a single person.

The other fallacy is that the work to be done on any given day will be neatly divided equally between the two partners. Wouldn't that be nice? It sounds great, but it never seems to work that way. And the thought that is should work that way is what creates a great deal of resentment between two people trying to love one another.

I have yet to meet a woman that hasn't felt as though she does more than her husband, and that may be true. It's been proven that women are better able to navigate between multiple things at once, while men tend to focus on one thing at a time. There's an argument that could be made that although men might accomplish fewer tasks than women, the quality of the work they're doing is better because they're more focused.

The simple truth is that it's the expectation that it should be equal that causes us unnecessary difficulties in our marriages. We begin keeping a mental scorecard to track all that we do to justify our position, blame our overwhelm on our partners, and track the mounting resentments.

But none of that serves us or our relationships.

We could choose to see it differently.

What if you both do as much as you can, as well as you can?

Maybe you're able to do more in terms of quantity? Maybe he's able to do things you cannot do and considers that to be his contribution? Maybe it's not ever going to be perfectly equal?

Marriage isn't always equal. There are times when one partner needs to carry more of the load and extend the other a bit of grace. And there will always be times when the other partner does much of the heavy lifting.

My client Cathy felt like she was doing everything in the relationship. If asked, she could give you a full rundown of all that she did around the house and while raising their children. Then, when her brother was diagnosed with cancer, all of her energy and attention went to being there for him. During that time, her husband showed up for her – and her brother – in a big way, providing extra support during a difficult time.

Expectations, particularly those we have of other people, almost always lead to disappointment and discord, since no one was put on this planet to meet our expectations (even our spouses). And a scorecard is not only unnecessary, but it also serves as a point of separation rather than a way for improving connection and understanding.

Selfishness

The dictionary defines selfish as *lacking consideration for others; concerned chiefly with one's own profit or pleasure.* That definition, however, implies that when we take care of our own needs, we automatically have a disregard for others and that other people suffer. But that's not always true. The two ideas are not mutually exclusive or diametrically opposed. You can actually take care of your needs without disregarding everyone else. It's the proverbial airline instructions of putting your own air mask on first before helping others. Apparently we either need a new definition of selfishness or we need a new word that will define taking care of your own needs so that you are better equipped to also care for and give to others.

I not only disagree, I also think this is how we were designed, and we should stop fighting it or thinking it should be otherwise. I'll explain.

If you don't take care of yourself, you will eventually feel depleted and when that happens, you have nothing of value to give anyone else. When you're endlessly giving to everyone else, without also giving to yourself, you will eventually feel depleted, like a gas tank that's on empty. We need to refill our own tanks if we're ever going to give someone a ride to where they want to go.

We are always teaching others how to treat us, based upon how we treat ourselves. When we play the martyr and pretend as though we have no needs or that everyone else is more important, we shouldn't be surprised when our needs do not get met. Why would we ever expect someone to do for us something that we're not willing to do for ourselves? Women learned to do this more than men because we have traditionally been the caretakers and nurturers, but it has evolved into nurturing at the expense to ourselves. And then we feel resentment since no one is taking care of our needs, so we are suffering unnecessarily. We are suffering as a result of our own actions and decisions because we were taught that putting everyone else before ourselves was the noble or nice thing to do. It's what would make everyone else more comfortable. Doing what our parents wanted us to do (rather than what we instinctively felt that we needed) is how we received their love and approval. This is how we learned.

We are all selfishly motivated. We just don't like to admit it because of the current definition. When we come into this world as a baby, we do not care about awakening our sleep-deprived parents in the middle of the night in order to get our needs met (hungry or diaper changed). When you ask a five-year-old if they want to go to the park and play, they never say, "No thank you, I haven't been a good boy and done all the things you asked me to do today, Mom." Instead, what you'll hear is, "Yes! And then can we go to the toy store? And then can we get ice cream? Can I stay up late tonight?" We come into this world selfishly motivated. What we learn is that everyone else's needs are more important than our own (and that somehow makes us virtuous).

Our nature – by design – is to be selfishly motivated. It is our responsibility to express what we need (the baby crying in the middle of the night) so that we can get our needs met. This idea that we should place everyone else's needs before our own was designed by someone who probably was trying to get their needs met by someone else.

Think about this for a second: The person that tells you, "You're so selfish," is telling you that because you're not meeting their needs first. So who exactly is it that's being selfish again?

This is our nature. This is how it's supposed to work. We each take care of our own needs and when we do, we are better equipped to help others that might need some help, love, and support from us. Nothing has gone wrong. Sometimes, I think God giggles at our interpretations of what was given to us.

Here's how this applies to your marriage:

You're upset with your beloved because he's not meeting your needs. He's busy meeting his own needs and seeing life through his lens from his perspective. How selfish of him! He's off meeting his needs, but you think he should be busy meeting your needs. That's not his job.

His job is to meet his needs.

Your job is to meet your needs.

That's when two people stop leaning on one another from a place of lack and depletion and truly begin supporting one another from a place of love and abundance.

When we fill our own cup first, we finally, mercifully, have something to give.

Selfishness isn't bad. Martyrdom is debilitating.

And we've got an entire generation (maybe two generations) that need to unlearn this.

Adults Get to Do What They Want

My step-daughter recently graduated high school, started college courses, and began working full-time. She's not getting enough sleep, has to keep up on her coursework, and has to pay for many of the things she wants for herself. She doesn't have much time to be with her friends or see her boyfriend. She calls this "adulting" and says it's hard.

She's right.

It is hard.

Gone now are the days of carefree play, where most of our needs are met by someone else, and even a few of our wants. As an adult, we have to figure out how to pay the bills. We have to carry the stress of careers, achieving our goals, raising children, caring for aging parents, and taking care of a residence. It's stressful – all this adulting – but there is one enormous benefit (which is also an enormous responsibility):

You get to do what you want to do.

No one can tell you what to do (although they try).

No one can force you to do anything (although we tell ourselves that).

No one can make you feel anything you don't want to feel (without your permission).

Every adult gets to do whatever they want to do, and they also get to live with the consequences of their choices.

That can be freeing or intimidating, depending upon how you look at it. It's yours to create and it's your responsibility.

As an adult, you get to do whatever you want.

Don't want to pay taxes? That's fine, but you'll go to jail.

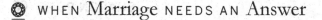

Don't want to put time, energy, and love into your marriage? That's okay, but do not expect it to last, feel good, or even magically thrive on its own.

Don't want to forgive? That's your choice, but you're the only one carrying the weight of the resentment.

We get to do what we want. We get to feel how we want to feel (now that you know it is your thoughts that create your feelings, not the circumstances). And we live with the outcome of our choices. It's probably the only benefit to this whole adulting thing. So we need to stop playing the victim in our own lives, stop telling ourselves the story that we didn't have a choice, and we need to stop trying to force others to do what we want them to do.

Both are lies, both cause unnecessary suffering, and both will destroy intimacy and connection in a relationship.

Grown-ups get to do whatever they want to do – and they get to live with the outcomes of those choices.

Some People Are Easy to Love

My niece has always been easy to love. As a child, she would pat my back with her tiny little hand when I held her in my arms because she learned that's what you do when you're held. As a teenager, she never hung up the phone without saying, "love you, bye!" Now, as a young adult, it's not unusual for her to call me in the morning just to let me know that she hopes I have a great day.

She's easy to love.

Wouldn't it be nice if everyone did the things that made them easy to love?

Wouldn't it be great if your husband would do all the things you would like so that he became easy to love? It would, for sure.

Again, it's lovely when that happens, but most days it doesn't feel so effortless.

That's because we've become conditioned to love when people point their love at us. We're not taught how to love and be loving when something other than love is pointed at us. That's how we learn to love conditionally and it's the basis for all of the long-term issues and feelings of disappointment in our marriages.

Our job is to love.

It's who we are; it's our true nature.

To love and to be loved is all we're here to do.

And we do it selfishly.

Yes, I said it....

We love so that we can feel good as we move through our lives.

We love so that we can take responsibility for how we feel and our own happiness.

Loving will always feel better than judging or nagging or hating. So love for purely selfish reasons and when you do, I promise that those around you will feel the impact of that love.

STEP FIVE: COMMUNICATION AS THE PATH TO CONNECTION

"When we avoid difficult conversations, we trade short-term discomfort for long-term dysfunction."
– Peter Bromberg

One of the most direct paths to connection (or reconnection) with your spouse is through communication. This is probably no surprise. What should surprise you, however, is that we're able to communicate anything at all to one another given how complex and difficult communication can be.

There are essentially two parts to all communication:

1. What we mean and what we say
2. What the other person hears and what they make it mean

Remember playing the telephone game when you were a kid where the whole class was in one big line whispering what was said to you by the person on your right to the person on your left? By the time the game was over and the sentence had reached the end of the line of kids, what the last person said didn't sound much like the initial sentence that started the telephone chain.

That's a very simplistic way of seeing how easy it is for communication issues to occur. But it's actually so much more difficult than that.

What we mean and what we say: We don't often get clear about what it is we are really feeling before the words begin to come out of our mouths. It certainly would be easier if we said what we really meant. It's the most direct path to take. But instead, we say what makes us feel right, justified, or safe.

For instance, let's say your son was supposed to be home by 11:00 and it's 11:20 when he walks through the door. You were worried and began hoping he was safe. But instead of saying, "I was starting to worry, I'm so glad you are okay," you say, "Where have you been? Why didn't you call?"

This is the first point of breakdown in communication: not saying what it is we actually mean. When we put up our guard and use criticism or sarcasm as a disguise for how we really feel, we're not being truthful.

What the other person hears and what they make it mean: The person on the receiving end of what you're attempting to communicate has their own lens, so they hear the series of words strung together and their mind gives those words meaning and context based upon what's embedded in their lens of past experiences, fears, insecurities, and beliefs.

Your son hears the words: *Where have you been? Why didn't you call?* Eight simple words and he makes that mean: *She doesn't trust me. She treats me like a child.* The conclusion he comes to is some version of, *I've gotta get out of here. I can't wait until I graduate.*

He begins to defend himself because he feels like he's being treated like a child, the two of you argue, and the issue escalates. You, as the parent, get frustrated and send him to his room – further cementing the idea that he's being treated like a child and needs to get away (from the metaphorical pillow over his face).

This is why I think it's amazing that we are actually able to communicate with one another at all. Plus, communication isn't getting easier when we take away most of the context that conveys meaning.

Lost in Translation

Dr. Albert Mehrabian, author of *Silent Messages*, found that only 7% of any message is conveyed through the words we use. The remaining 93% is comprised of certain vocal elements (such as tone and cadence) and non-verbal elements (such as facial expressions, hand gestures and posture).

Communication is difficult enough when we are speaking directly to one another, but it is virtually impossible to convey our true sentiment when we remove all the vocal and non-verbal elements of communication.

Technology has helped us in some ways and hurt us in others, as we communicate more and more through text messaging, even the most difficult and painful aspects of our relationships. Many couples are struggling with communication now because they're relying extensively on communication through text messages, which literally removes 93% of the context to what it is you're trying to communicate. We've begun to rely on texting with our spouses because we tell ourselves:

- We're able to think through what we want to say before it comes out of our mouths
- There's a record of what was said (but we cannot hear what's not being said)
- The emotion is removed from the communication. (But you cannot remove the emotion the receiver will feel when reading the text based upon the thoughts they have about it and the lens through which they interpret it.).

While there's a small element of truth in those beliefs, the price being paid to rely so heavily on texting as a primary means of communication – particularly about the really difficult conversations in our most intimate relationships – is higher than the perceived benefits. If we're really honest with ourselves, the reasons we rely heavily on text messages for the important conversations with our spouses is because it feels easier to text than to speak it aloud. It's a way of hiding, which only serves to weaken the relationship.

You're Only Responsible for Yourself

We can only ever be responsible for ourselves, how we communicate, and how we receive and interpret what's being communicated from others. We can each get better about expressing what it is we really mean and the message and feelings we want to convey. And we can get better about consciously choosing how we interpret what people are communicating to us.

A client of mine, who I'll refer to as Valerie, had been married for thirty-two years and, for at least the last ten years, had struggled to make it work with her husband. When she reached out to me, her husband had told her a few days prior that he was done and wanted a divorce. This wasn't the first time she had heard the "D" word from him, but somehow, she thought this time was different, and it scared her.

It's not as though Valerie was surprised to discover that things hadn't been going well between them; anyone could see it. One evening, after too many cocktails, for both of them, the police were even called to their home in the Hamptons because the arguing had turned physical. That was the breaking point for both of them. Something had to change. He thought the only way was to exit the marriage, but Valerie wanted to learn how to tackle issues in a loving and respectful manner without feeling fearful or intimidated. She also wanted to stop absorbing the blame and anger that she felt was being tossed at her.

Through our work together, Valerie was able to address the difficult topics with her husband. They were finally able to talk to – and really hear – one another. She stopped walking on eggshells so that she could try to express her feelings in a way that wouldn't disrupt him or make him angry. Instead, she got really clear about what she was feeling (step one: know what you're feeling) and then she communicated those feelings (step two: tell your partner how you feel) without expectations of how he should respond. She simply shared what was authentic and important for her to share. The minute she stopped worrying about his reaction to what was true for her, she was able to express herself more freely, and he was free to interpret her words through his own lens. She couldn't control his interpretation of her feelings, but she could be open, loving, and authentic.

Valerie and her husband are now happier than they've ever been. They're no longer arguing.

They're being loving, respectful, and even flirtatious with one another again. They've both re-engaged and recommitted to the relationship in a new way.

Keeping Only What Is Ours

We have precious little ability to control how our partners are receiving and interpreting what we're saying, but when we understand how communication works, we can see what's happening and course-correct before it goes down a long, winding path, and you're scratching your head thinking, *how did we get here?*

I'll give you a very personal example between my husband and myself:

My husband had been a firefighter and paramedic for seventeen years. When we met and married, he loved his job. He loved helping people, and he was good at it. He didn't just transport people to the hospital, he talked to them about what they were experiencing, and he encouraged them through their struggle. He liked working in the low-income area of Dayton, Ohio, because he knew he was making a difference. He even won a Medal of Valor for his heroic attempt to save children from a burning home.

The days of firefighters sitting around watching television, cooking chili, and working out while waiting for the next fire are long gone. Now that they are also the local paramedics, they run from one drug overdose to another, and one emergency to another, all day and all night long. They run on adrenaline, with very little food and almost no rest.

When Derrick's shift was working for twenty-four hours straight, although far from easy, he had acclimated to resting during the day on his off days so that he could do it all again every three days. We, as a couple, navigated our way through that challenge as well, and it became routine for us.

But the city changed their schedule. Now, instead of working for twenty-four hours straight on very little food and little rest, Derrick would be required to work a minimum of forty-eight hours straight, sometimes longer.

Understand that my husband is a health fanatic and is in incredibly good shape. He doesn't put anything artificial into his body ever and used to run the stairs in our twenty story condo building for exercise. And this new schedule essentially brought this man to his knees physically and mentally within one year.

Derrick's sleep schedule was an absolute disaster; running on adrenaline while at work and crashing for many hours during the day while at home. Because he had no regular sleep schedule even when he was off, his body couldn't catch-up to provide him the rest every human body needs to function well. The physical exhaustion also made the mental and emotional pieces of his job much more difficult. Now, when a child died in a fire or he had to pronounce a teenager dead from a gunshot wound, the images stayed with him longer and haunted him. He became irritable and frustrated with me because, of course, I couldn't understand what was being asked of him. (I had never stayed up and worked non-stop saving peoples' lives for forty-eight hours+ at a time.) I just wanted my old husband back. This new schedule was rapidly taking a toll on him, and us.

Derrick began talking about leaving his career and walking away from being a firefighter and paramedic. He began thinking about starting his own health and nutrition company.

This threw me into a bit of a mental tailspin.

I was running a growing coaching practice and the life of an entrepreneur is not one of safety and security, so I always thought that even though I made more money than Derrick, he was the responsible one, the one carrying the health insurance, the one saving for our future, the one with all the stability. I could be more carefree because I believed he was more grounded.

The immediate thoughts that came to mind (and out of my mouth) were some version of:

Who's going to be the responsible one?

Will I have to give up my coaching practice and get a job again?

Will we have health insurance?

Who's going to save for our retirement?

Will we be okay?

What Derrick's mind heard and made my words mean was that I didn't believe in him. I didn't believe that he could go out on his own and be successful. And when I looked closely, he was right...but it didn't have anything to do with him. It had everything to do with some unconscious programming within myself.

Whenever I feel fearful, I get curious about it because I know that fear is not our natural state. When I looked a little deeper at my fears, I realized these were old childhood wounds that I had unconsciously carried.

As I mentioned in my introduction, it was a fairly common occurrence in my home growing up that my father, who was in hotel management, would either quit his job without another one lined up or get fired. He would often talk about working for himself, but he never did. We would often go from being fine financially to insecurity and hardship during those times of transition. And almost every time this happened, it meant the family would need to move to a new city and my brother and I would move to a new school. My brain easily made that mean that when someone quit their job without another one lined up, we weren't okay financially.

My fears were being triggered from old wounds:

Someone had to be stable in the relationship (and at the time, I wasn't thinking that was me...).

Stability meant being employed by someone else, rather than self-employed.

When the man of the home quit his job it led to insecurity and instability. It meant the woman had to work harder to support them both. It meant struggle and hardship.

And a sneaky little thought that had crept into my experience was that, *As a woman, you cannot rely on a man to take care of you.* Oh, that was a nasty thought hidden beneath the surface. But once I could identify it, I could see how it had completely played out in my life over and over and over again.

Here's the good news: Now that I could see the thoughts that were causing the fearful reactions, I was able to make conscious choices about whether or not I wanted to keep those thoughts. Clearly, I did not, so I did my own work to believe something different. I changed my thoughts to ones that were far more productive (and certainly better for my relationship with my husband):

We've always had everything we needed. We've always figured out how to pay our bills. Why would this be any different?

We're incredibly smart and talented people, money is just an energetic exchange of those gifts and contributions. And we have many gifts and ways to contribute to the world.

One of the things that will make or break you as an entrepreneur is your level of belief in yourself and your own abilities. Derrick wanted to start his own business and one thing he always had was an unwavering belief in himself. It's actually one of the things I admire most about him.

My fears softened enough so that when the time came, I was able to be the loving and supportive woman he needed me to be. Derrick walked through the door one Sunday morning after a long shift looking like the walking dead. He ate some breakfast and went to bed for several hours. When he woke up, he showered, and told me he was going to the lake. That, I knew, was code for *I have some thinking to do.* I asked what was going on and he said to me: "I'm going to leave my job and I need to figure out how to manage your anxiety."

Now, I was able to respond with, "Go think about what you want to do and what you need to do. Managing my anxiety is my job, not yours. We'll talk when you get home."

When we had the opportunity to talk later, that's when he shared with me that the fears I had expressed about him leaving his job left him feeling like I didn't believe in him. I said words like, "Who's going to carry the health insurance," but what his mind made that mean was that his wife didn't believe in him.

Now I had the opportunity to course-correct given the self-discovery work I had done for myself. I was able to show up as the wife he needed me to be and as the woman I wanted to be in that defining moment.

I had a yoga teacher that reminded us in every class, "Your world right now is only 24 inches wide by 68 inches long (the size of a yoga mat). For the next sixty minutes, that's all you need to focus upon and that is your only responsibility." That gentle reminder she provided reminded me that when I focus on only what is mine and what is right in front of me at that moment, that it's all manageable. It's only when I try to wrap my mind around things much larger – or worse, things that were never mine to manage in the first place – that it becomes overwhelming.

We don't have control over how others interpret our words, but when we see that their interpretation doesn't align with our intention, we can get curious about that discrepancy and course-correct as needed.

Communication Differences Between Men and Women

There are known and proven differences in the ways that men and women communicate with one another.

In the book *For Women Only*, Shaunti Feldhahn talks about how men and women's brains process information differently. Women, because they have lots of connections between the left and right hemispheres of the brain, can process information quickly. We literally will talk our way through a problem to quickly identify the right solution. This is why when there's an issue between couples, it's the woman who wants to sit down and talk about it as the path to resolution.

Men, on the other hand, are internal processors. Their brains are wired to process one thing at a time. That's why it's not uncommon for men to need to step away and think something through (go deep into this one issue) before being able to come to a resolution.

There have been a wide number of studies showing that women possess a larger vocabulary, process information, and speak faster, literally using more words every day than men do. Our communication style is more interactive than men's, and we are better equipped to listen with empathy and notice emotions.

And likewise, there are a number of things that men are naturally better at than women, such as problem solving, being direct and to-the-point, and even excelling at some mental tasks.

Science has told us that we evolved this way from the days of when men had to hunt for food and women stayed back to take care of the community and the family. During that time, communication was simply much less necessary for men – even potentially scaring off the prey. Communication is a skill that has been cultivated in women for thousands of years, but not to the same degree in men.

So, not only is the female brain wired differently than the male brain, we've cultivated the skill of communication over the course of thousands of years.

Communication is our go-to solution as women because it's where we excel and are comfortable. But just because that's where we naturally excel doesn't mean that it's the only path to problem solving, connection, and even creating intimacy.

Problem Solving

Every couple is going to encounter problems that need to be resolved, and to do so, at some point, communication and listening are going to need to play a role. This might mean that there are steps to a solution.

For instance, one of my clients was married to a man with a great deal of fear about money, so whenever she spent money it triggered anxiety in him and then typically a big argument between them. His fear led him to try to control her behavior. His solution was to have 100% control over their finances, and he would give her an allowance. He also wanted her commitment that she would not buy specific things without gaining his agreement first. Obviously, this was not going to work for my client. It felt like the proverbial pillow over the face: controlling, distrusting, and even hostile.

She wanted to talk about it. She wanted to address each issue, but he couldn't hear her through his noisy, fearful mind. So instead of attempting to wrestle it to the ground in one conversation, she decided to tell her husband what was true for her and then gave him the opportunity to step away and attempt to come up with an alternative solution – one that would work for both of them.

She was not willing to be in a relationship where one person had all financial control. She was not willing to be in an intimate relationship where there was no trust or freedom. Her suggestion that she wanted him to step away and consider was to (1) have a joint account for the joint bills and (2) each have their own separate accounts that they could spend as they wished. That gave her the freedom she needed and made her feel like an equal partner in the marriage. When he had time to consider it, that approach met his need for security and removed his need to micromanage and control her behavior. Plus, there was the added bonus of not having to blow up their lives, their marriage, and invest thousands in lawyers dividing up their assets between them.

Women can talk through a problem, navigating emotions and circumstances, to quickly come to a solution. Men sometimes need to step away and think it through before coming to a solution that works for them. My client got what she needed, and she gave him the time he needed to feel comfortable with the solution.

Creating Connection

When we want to increase the intimacy we feel in our marriages, most of the time women want more communication. And that's understandable since that's where we're comfortable. But just because that's a skill within us that comes naturally, why have we decided that men need to show love for us in only that one way?

Modern psychology suggests that communication is the path to intimacy. But given our respective histories regarding communication, that also implies then that men are going to struggle with intimacy, which isn't necessarily the case. They just might struggle with delivering on the promise of intimacy in their marriages through the single portal of communication.

What I'm suggesting here is that maybe communication isn't always the best – and certainly not the only – answer to increasing intimacy within the marriage. Maybe there can be many paths to intimacy when each partner is able to allow the other to express it in the way that feels good for them.

Much like the concepts expressed in Gary Chapman's book, *The Five Love Languages*, there is no one right way to show love and there is no singular right way to cultivate intimacy. So the most important thing to know is how your partner expresses love and attempts to cultivate connection with you.

Maybe it's by taking something off your plate that he knows is difficult or feels like drudgery for you. Or maybe it's when he surprises you with a sweet card, a thank you, or a lingering kiss. Once you know how your spouse is attempting to establish a closer connection with you, you're better equipped to notice and appreciate those efforts.

And for the husbands who genuinely want to cultivate a more intimate relationship with their spouses, but know that long, in-depth conversations aren't their strong suits, here are a few other ideas for them:

- Find one thing to appreciate about her each day and tell her. Thank her for making a delicious meal. Tell her how her eyes light up when she's happy. Tell her you appreciate her continuing to laugh at your jokes, even after all these years. Tell her she's beautiful.

- Be present for one another. When she's speaking – since communication is important for her – look her in the eyes, really listen without worrying about what you should say, put down the phone and turn off the television.

- Create something together that feels fun for both of you. Cook a meal together, take a class together, complete a project around the house that you've both wanted to do for a while, or plan a vacation together. Coming together to create something new that didn't exist previously is a fun way to feel more connected to one another. My husband and I have a saying, "At the end of the day, I'm on Team Pope." That's a sense that we're on the same team and working toward shared goals brings us closer. It keeps us focused on what's important.

I love when I am able to coach therapists because I can ask them more direct questions and move more quickly with them at times than other clients. I also learn different things from them, as I did from my client, Anne. She said that we carry emotions in the body, but we process emotions in the brain. Therefore, if you're having a discussion with your husband and you want him to really hear and connect with you, touch him on the arm or hold his hand as you're speaking. That physical touch can do more to ground a man than words alone.

Communication can be a great way to amplify intimacy within a marriage, but it doesn't have to be the only way to do so. If one or both of you struggles with emotions, vulnerability, and communication, there are other ways to feel closer to your beloved.

STEP SIX: YOUR BUSINESS AND BOUNDARIES

"There is a difference between having good boundaries and creating barriers. Boundaries are like a fence with a gate – the energy can come and go – because you've made those clear declarations; barriers are like a shield you drag around – ready to defend yourself from attacks."
– Danielle LaPorte

One of the greatest spiritual teachers of our time is a woman named Byron Katie. Most people refer to her as Katie. Through her work (which she calls *The Work*), she teaches that there are only three types of business in the universe: mine, yours, and God's. And every situation can only fall into one of those categories at any given time.

My business is composed of only the things that I can control in my experience: my choices, actions, behaviors, how I feel, and to a certain degree, the thoughts I create about my experience.

Your business is composed of only the things that others can control in their own experiences: their choices, actions, behaviors, how they feel, and to a (much more limited) degree, the thoughts they create about their experiences.

God's business is all the things that no one can control. I put the weather in this category, when the sun rises and sets, I put wars in this category, and the last day I will walk this planet. I cannot control any of those things. (Feel free to replace the title of God with *The Universe, Source, Higher Power* or whatever you use to describe the energy that raises the sun each day and places the stars in the sky each night.)

We spend far too much time outside of our own business. We're busy handing out unsolicited advice or thinking that we know how others should think, feel, behave, or believe. We spend inordinate amounts of time trying to convince the people around us to see life through our lens or approach life the way we would. Funny enough, we even spend time in God's business thinking that the weather should be different than the reality of what it actually is. Every time there's a natural disaster or in my case, the weather drops below 50 degrees, I think it should be different.

"You should eat healthier foods." Not your business.

"My husband should be better at managing his time." Not my business.

"Living in Florida, I will have to deal with hurricanes." Not my business.

"My mother-in-law should be nicer." Not your business.

"My child should respect me." (Believe it or not...) Not your business.

There are two tragic things that occur when we choose to not remain solely in our own business:

1. We're causing ourselves unnecessary suffering. Trying to control the uncontrollable (that includes your husband and everyone else around you) will always feel like a losing battle. To me, it's the equivalent of beating your head against a wall. Eventually, all you get is a headache.

2. Secondly, and maybe more importantly, when we're over in someone else's business, no one

is there for us, our journey, and our business. Just like we cannot be in two different places at the same time, nor can we simultaneously be in someone else's business and our own business at the same time. When we're over attempting to live our spouse's life for them, we're not living and existing in our own lives, which are truly our only jobs.

I know you understand this intellectually, but I promise that putting it into practice in your life consistently is much more difficult. Sometimes, we avoid remaining in our own business because we don't want to deal with what's there. Our own business can be too painful or difficult to deal with, so instead we avoid it by submerging ourselves in other people's drama (what I like to call, OPD). It's so much easier to tell other people how to live than it is to live that way myself. As a coach, I call this "eating my own dog food."

My new client, Virginia, was sharing with me the story about her husband, Alan. Alan had been a mechanical engineer for the last forty years and was now retired. Virginia was really irritated with him because he was sitting around the house saying he was bored, but not doing anything. He talked occasionally about getting a new hobby or volunteering, but had yet to pursue either. The painful thought Virginia was harboring was that he should be busy, or active, or productive, particularly because she was so stressed with everything that existed on her own plate. She said, "The last thing I need is to be responsible for his happiness now." Alan was not asking her to take responsibility for him or his happiness. She was unsuccessfully attempting to do that on her own. And remaining in his business, thinking he should do something different than what he was doing was only aggravating her, causing unnecessary suffering. He was fine. He might have been a little bored, but he was not irritated or aggravated. As long as she was in his business she was suffering and she was not simultaneously able to be there for herself to manage what was on her plate: her choices, actions, and behaviors. Virginia resented Alan for not being busier, while she kept taking on more and more responsibilities herself that left her feeling exhausted and overwhelmed. He didn't make those choices, she did. And she made those choices because she wasn't paying attention to what she most needed.

You'll know you're in someone else's business when you feel frustrated, powerless, angry, or any similar negative emotion. When you find yourself there, stop and ask yourself, "Whose business am I in right now?" Be willing to see how you're not in your own business and resist the temptation to justify your need for being in their business. Instead, just use that phrase as an opportunity to turn your focus back to what is yours, because that's where all your power lives and your peace resides. That's where you can make decisions that honor you and let everyone else off the hook.

Setting Boundaries

You might think that there is no place for boundaries in your closest, most intimate relationship, but that's not true. Boundaries are a necessary part of every relationship, but just like no one taught us how to be in relationship with one another, no one taught us how to set boundaries well either.

As young girls, we were taught to be nice and to be agreeable, not to make waves or express an opinion. Even as we grew older, we were directly or indirectly told to place our needs and desires on the back burner and take care of others instead. That is especially true after having children. This felt in alignment with who we are because we are nurturers by nature. Women will go years – or even decades – without setting healthy boundaries that honor their own needs and preferences, because no one's ever taught them how to do it (or given them permission).

Conversely, it was considered a sign of strength in young men when they would express their opinions or stand up for themselves. This is why men tend to have fewer issues with knowing how to set boundaries than do women.

Why We Avoid Setting Boundaries

When we think of setting boundaries, we often think of it as putting up a wall, establishing a metaphorical line that is not to be crossed. And of course, that is one way of setting a boundary. But that hard line is the very reason why most women hesitate to do it.

We worry that if we set boundaries, people won't like us.

If we express what we need and want, people will call us selfish.

If we set healthy boundaries, others will think we're bitchy or bossy.

One of the reasons we avoid setting boundaries is because we think it needs to be delivered with "edge."

Edge looks like anger...

It sounds like sarcasm...

Edge feels like having to shove something down someone's throat that we assume they do not want...which will never feel good.

The thought that it has to be loud or rude to get someone's attention isn't true. As a matter of fact, I could argue the opposite.

Have you ever seen a public speaker all of a sudden go silent or begin to whisper in the middle of their presentation? They do that because it gets your attention. It's an attention-grabbing technique that makes you lean into what they're saying. The same is true for setting boundaries; sometimes a quiet but firm "No, that doesn't work for me" is far more powerful than a loud roar.

We Can't Resent a Boundary We Never Set

My client, Anita, had what some might refer to as a monster-in-law, rather than a mother-in-law. Out of respect, I will simply refer to her as Barbara. Barbara was living with Anita's family, where all of her physical needs were being met and where she was able to sustain a close relationship with her grandchildren. But Barbara had some opinions about what constituted a good wife and mother for her son. She was from a different generation and had some ideas and opinions that she wasn't shy about sharing.

If you were a good mother, you would be home more for your children and make sure they're eating and dressing properly.

Good wives make sure that the house is kept clean at all times.

Let me make that (referring to a specific dish my client was cooking). I know how to do it better than you do.

Anita felt like an abused prisoner in her own home. Barbara was overbearing with the children, the cooking, and the cleaning, oftentimes taking over her kitchen and being outwardly critical of Anita. Mind you, Anita was a kind and caring mother and a loving and (very understanding) wife, but she was also an ER doctor, so when the house wasn't spotless, she didn't sweat it. No one was dying. She had never defined her worthiness or quality of being a wife by whether or not the laundry was folded perfectly or if there was a spot on her floor. She's like most working mothers, just trying to keep her head above water and her children happy and safe.

She complained to me about the things her mother-in-law would say to her, and while I agreed with her that Barbara was out of line, as her coach, I also challenged her because she had never set boundaries with her mother-in-law. You don't get the right to resent boundaries being crossed that were never set in the first place. You should fully expect that the treatment you allow for yourself – either good or bad – will continue until you let them know otherwise. If you want someone to get to the right destination, you should give them the map.

Whenever Barbara would say hurtful things, Anita just took it. She was taught at a young age to not talk back to her parents or other adults. Plus, her husband wasn't sticking up for her (which is another issue entirely), and she didn't want to cause an argument between she and her husband. This was his mother, after all. She thought the answer was to go to her husband and convince him to set a boundary with his mother that he had never set previously, but that wasn't happening, and his lack of engagement only caused more issues between them as a couple. It was time to put her big girl pants on.

Anita needed to choose between her only two (good) options:

Take the path of least resistance, not paying any mind to what her mother-in-law said and did. (This is a ninja move and you have to be very well versed at staying in your business and managing your personal energy. It's very difficult, but is possible.)

Or alternatively, she could begin to set boundaries with her mother-in-law.

It's important to note here that the only people we really need to set boundaries with are those that don't readily recognize or respect other people's boundaries. If you and I were living with Anita, we wouldn't be behaving as her in-law was because we are aware of healthy personal boundaries. The problem is created when we ignore or overlook the disregard for our own personal boundaries with someone who is not aware or respectful of them.

Expressing What's Not Okay

If you are a human being on this planet, you have a right to your own personal boundaries, needs, desires, and preferences. None of this makes you unreasonable or selfish. It makes you a human being.

When someone crosses a line with you, it's important to make them aware that a personal boundary of yours has been crossed. They're not mind readers, so at least initially give them the benefit of the doubt that they didn't realize they were overstepping. You can let them know by using phrases, such as:

I'm not okay with that.

That doesn't work for me.

Please don't do that again.

This gives them the rules of engagement on being in relationship with you. Rather than thinking of it as building a wall, think of it as a map to the treasure. They now know what won't work (and therefore, what will work) if they want to be in a healthy relationship with you going forward.

When you have to tell someone *no*, do you find yourself justifying your reason for saying *no*? Maybe you're like me and you've made up little white lies that would explain why you are not going to do something that someone else wants you to do. Instead, just for fun, next time someone asks you to do something that you don't want to do, practice saying only the word *no*, or *No, thank you*. Use the word *no* as a complete sentence. It's incredibly empowering. It will feel awkward as hell at first because it's not something you're used to doing. But if you cannot say *no* to someone without justifying or explaining the reason for your *no*, you will never be able to stand up to the mother-in-law and check her when she's out of line while living under your roof AND maintain a healthy relationship with her.

A Word to the Wise...

Remember how I told you that the only people you will need to set boundaries with are those that aren't aware of or respectful of other people's boundaries? Well, it's many of those same people that you will have to make aware of your boundaries more than once. If you think expressing what's not okay with you only one time will magically do the trick, you're going to be disappointed (and likely give up, assuming it's a losing battle). Instead, go into setting that first boundary with the assumption that this will be the first of many reminders they will need to change the way they engage with you.

Dr. Maya Angelou said, "You teach people how to treat you." I fully believe that's true. And if you've been historically teaching someone that their behavior is okay with you by not telling them otherwise, why in the world would you expect that behavior to automatically change after a single communication? You shouldn't.

Maybe you're in a situation like my client Anita, where the bad behavior by Barbara, her mother-in-law, had gone on for so long she was doubtful it would ever change, leaving her feeling trapped and powerless. When Anita was willing to gently and lovingly change the rules of engagement with Barbara by consistently telling her, "That doesn't work for me," "That's not okay with me," and even, "I treat you respectfully and I expect the same from you in my own home," eventually things started to shift. Barbara began to notice. She didn't like it, but she took notice. That's okay.

You'll be happy to know that Anita also sought out the help of a cleaning service, a part-time nanny and a meal prep service so that she could focus on the roles that were important to her, such as being an amazing ER doctor and showing up as the woman and mother she wanted to be in her life and with her children. The other things that were less important to Anita, such as cooking and cleaning, would still get done but were no longer considered her responsibility and she was able to side-step the judgement from her mother-in-law rather than get her mother-in-law to change her long-held values. I've never heard of a cleaning service saving a marriage, but sometimes choosing the path of least resistance is also the wisest option.

How Is It Serving You?

We only do the things that serve us in some way, shape, or form. Others overstepping with you has served them in some way. Maybe it's helped them to get their needs met or maybe, like Barbara, it's helped them to feel a little more right or righteous in their own lives to point out the apparent flaws in others. The reason is less important than the consistency you show in changing the rules of engagement when setting new boundaries in your relationships.

Anyone who refuses to respect the boundaries that you have consistently set will not be able to remain in the same type of relationship with you moving forward. You are not obligated to allow everyone free rein in your life – even (and sometimes, especially) family. Sometimes the relationship needs to be redefined when boundaries cannot consistently be respected. And if you're not willing to make that stand for yourself, you will always struggle with boundaries.

Expressing What Is Okay (The Positive Side of Boundary Setting)

The day I fell in love with the topic of boundaries was the day I listened to a podcast from Terri Cole on the topic. She's the one that introduced me to the concept that boundaries are not only telling those around you what is not okay with you; it is also telling those around you what is okay with you. The positive side of boundary setting is sharing with people what you prefer and what you need.

The problem I see in relationships again and again is when we don't tell the people closest to us what we need or what we truly desire, but then assume they'll be able to meet our needs.

Mary put her needs on the back burner for thirty years. She raised three boys and her husband was a busy lawyer. She had a real estate business herself and was always the one to make sure all of her boys were well cared for. That loving care came easy for Mary because she was a kind and generous giver by nature and that always felt right and good for her as a mother and a wife.

But in making it all about everyone else, she had essentially taught her family that she either had no needs or that her needs were unimportant. So now when there was more time and space for her in her own life, she still wasn't getting her needs met – and she started to feel a little resentful about that, especially with her husband. She thought it was finally her turn, but no one else received that memo. She and her husband grew apart and her resentments were mounting.

Mary was changing the rules on her husband (and by the way, not really telling him). She had always taught him that her needs were unimportant based upon never expressing what she needed. But now she wanted her needs met – by him – and was disappointed when that didn't magically happen. If we cannot (or will not) express to our partners what we need, then we cannot honestly expect that those needs will be met.

When we don't tell people what we need, they are left to guess, and they will almost always guess incorrectly. Or, alternatively, they will give us what they would need. That will only fall short of your expectations about 99% of the time.

The other side of boundaries, I learned through Terri Cole, is telling those we love what is okay with us and what we need most, and when we do that, we are telling the truth of who we are and letting them really know us. We're letting them in. That floored me.

Think about that for a second: you can be married to someone for thirty years, but if you've never expressed your needs, desires, or preferences – do they really know you? Even if they love you, do they really know the person they think they love, or do they know and love the woman who has no needs or preferences of her own?

Your children may not even really know you. If you've oriented your life around their needs and preferences, never giving life to your own, do they really know you as a woman – or only as a selfless mother?

This, to me, was a game-changer. Expressing boundaries was no longer just the stuff we didn't really want to do – telling people what's not okay. Expressing the other side of boundaries was also letting people know the real you, the one with preferences all her own. It was telling the truth of who you are and letting the people you love to know you intimately.

Building a Muscle

If you're like my client, Mary, setting boundaries and telling people what you need is not something you were taught or something that comes naturally. Therefore, like anything new, you're going to need to practice it to become good at it.

If you walked into the gym for the first time, you wouldn't automatically walk over to the fifty-pound weight and attempt to pick it up. Instead, you would probably walk over to the five-pound weight and lift that for a week or two until that felt easy and manageable. Once that felt easy, then you would reach for the ten-pound weight. You would only reach for a fifty-pound weight once you had worked your way up to that. The same is true for setting boundaries. You will never be able to set the equivalent of the fifty-pound boundary with your mother-in-law if when asked what you want for dinner, your immediate response is, "I don't care…whatever you want." If you can't say no to something you genuinely don't want to do with the other moms, you'll never be able to tell your husband what you really need or desire in the bedroom.

This is a muscle you're building, so every time you flex it, you're strengthening it.

Each time you say "No" or "No, thank you" to something you don't want to do.

Each time you express your preference.

Each time you tell your husband what you need or desire.

Each time you tell your mother-in-law "Thank you, but I've got this."

Each time you say, "That's not okay with me," and mean it.

Those are all free-weight bicep curls getting you stronger and stronger so that when the big test comes, and you need to set an important and difficult boundary, you're strong enough to curl it.

What to Expect When You Begin Setting New Boundaries

I've already mentioned that the only people you will need to repeatedly set boundaries with are those that are not used to recognizing and respecting other people's boundaries. That means you cannot expect to say it once and expect everything to change. If it were that easy, most of us wouldn't struggle with this.

Here's the other important thing: When you begin setting new boundaries with people, they're going to notice. That might look like them thrashing about in some form of an adult temper-tantrum or it might just look like them stopping to notice that something has changed with interest or curiosity.

This is a good thing.

You're changing the rules of engagement. You want them to notice. They cannot change the way they engage with you if they don't notice that the rules have changed.

Setting boundaries and stating what doesn't work for you is your right as a human being on this planet. Everyone has the right to set personal boundaries for themselves. It's not wrong. It's not bad. It's telling people the rules of engagement: what works for being in a relationship with you and what does not work for being in a relationship with you. It's giving people the roadmap and I personally find that comforting. Some boundaries are obvious (or should be), while others are a personal preference that need to be shared so that people know the rules of how to engage with you. Either way, you'll never get your needs met if you do not know or cannot express what you need.

The Difficult Conversations

Many times when relationships feel tentative or unsteady, we avoid the most difficult conversations. We avoid those conversations to keep the peace. The problem is that often the conversations we avoid are those that we most need to have with our partners.

No one likes to have the difficult conversations. No one enjoys disagreements or arguments. And no one likes hearing the dreaded four words, "We need to talk."

But avoiding the difficult issues – even in the attempt to keep the peace – does not help you or your marriage.

Don't be afraid to say the things that most need to be said in your relationship. In my experience, problems that are ignored do not age well on their own. The resentments get bigger and the distance between you and your spouse widens. We might avoid the argument on a random Sunday night in order to keep the peace for the rest of the week, but in doing so, we avoid addressing the things that could change the marriage over the course of decades.

I knew my client was at the end of her rope and ready to call it quits in her marriage and I gently nudged her to have the long overdue talk with her husband. If she was almost ready to walk out the door, I think he deserved to know where her head was at. (I know I would want to know if my husband was at the point of leaving the marriage.) Here was our text conversation that Saturday afternoon:

Me: *It's getting to be about the time to have the talk darlin...*

Her: *I know but then he leans in and just tries harder to be endearing and it gets awkward. At least if I don't say anything, I don't have to deal with that.*

She went on to say:

We are alone together here at the house, but it feels even more alone...if that makes sense.

Trapped is my reality right now. I feel completely trapped.

My client – in that moment – was making the choice to remain trapped (her words) as to avoid feeling awkward with her husband. That seems like a lousy trade-off in my mind. She traded in a feeling of awkwardness for a moment and, in return, was willing to keep the feeling of trapped for a lifetime, or at least the foreseeable future.

This is what fear will have us do.

We will run from the discomfort in a moment, not realizing that in doing so, we're signing-up for a lifetime of unhappiness and heartache. No one would consciously choose that if given the options in that manner, but we choose it every single day when we avoid the most difficult conversations in our relationships.

The Ring of Fire

Sometimes these conversations – letting our spouses know how close we are to the edge of calling it quits – feel like walking right up to the Ring of Fire. The Ring of Fire is a concept by my mentor and teacher, Martha Beck, where she describes the

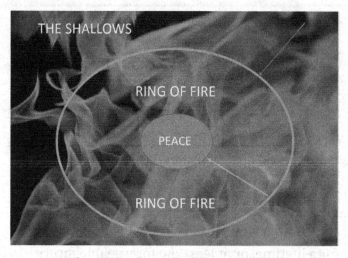

THE SHALLOWS

RING OF FIRE

PEACE

RING OF FIRE

process of moving through the most difficult things in our lives.

The Shallows: The Shallows is where most of us choose to stay because it feels safe. We never look too closely at what's lacking in our lives, we never rock the boat by expressing what we need most, and we certainly find value in making our lives look pretty good from the outside on Facebook, regardless of what they feel like on the inside.

The Place of Peace: Everyone wants to exist in the place of peace: knowing who we are, liking who we are, and carrying ourselves in a way that feels in integrity with that person. That's living in peace. Everyone wants that, but there's a reason why most don't have it. The reason is that in order to get to that place of peace, you have to be willing to walk through the Ring of Fire.

The Ring of Fire: The Ring of Fire is the difficult, awkward, and even terrifying parts of our lives that we avoid. We avoid those parts of our lives because they're uncomfortable (damn uncomfortable), sometimes feeling like we're literally being burned alive or walking on hot coals. Our minds that want to keep us safe tell us it's a horrible idea to walk through that fire. Instead, it's just easier to remain out in the Shallows.

The Ring of Fire can be something as simple as having a difficult or awkward conversation with your husband to something as terrifying as telling your husband you don't know what else to do and maybe the only answer is to give up the struggle and separate. Both feel impossible in the moment and so it's easy to see why most avoid this.

The Ring of Fire never feels good, but it's part of the process to get to a place of real peace.

She Wasn't Ready

The reason we avoid awkward for a moment in exchange for trapped for a lifetime is because we feel like we're not ready.

Not ready because it might turn into him trying harder and wanting to connect and that's just awkward for us both...

Not ready because it could turn into an argument and it's just easier to ignore it and have another glass of wine...

Not ready because frankly, we're just so damn tired of having these conversations and nothing ever changing...

There are only two reasons why people are ever willing to walk through the Ring of Fire:

1. They're either in so much pain that they absolutely have to find another way to provide them some relief (this is the equivalent and the motivation that accompanies hitting "rock bottom").

2. Their desire is so great that they cannot turn away from it.

- Entrepreneurs walk through a ring of fire to get their businesses off the ground because their desire is so strong.

- A mother who cannot swim will run into the ocean if she feels like her son is drowning because her desire for her son to be safe is stronger than her fear of drowning.

- And, for better or worse (pun intended), this is the reason why people will leave a horrible marriage when there's been an affair and someone else has ignited that desire and fills in all the gaps, making them feel the way they've always longed to feel. This other person has shown them what is possible, and it is that desire that now pulls them into The Ring of Fire.

This is simple human nature. We don't actively seek out change in our lives because change is scary and we have a built-in mechanism to help us avoid all things scary so that we can remain safe, secure, and stuck. It takes either a great deal of pain or a great desire to take that step from The Shallows into The Ring of Fire.

This is the single biggest reason I see for why women in unhappy marriages get stuck. They're not in great pain: their husband isn't beating them, it all looks pretty good from the outside, it's bearable, but not pleasurable. Plus, they don't have the great desire pulling them from the other end, so they convince themselves that they can be fine with fine, when they know in their hearts that what they have and the way they're existing in their relationships is far from fine.

No one is ever ready to walk through The Ring of Fire. There's never a good time to tell your husband you're close to giving up on your marriage. There's never a good time to admit to an affair (and I'm not entirely convinced that's productive). And likewise, there will never be the perfect time to have an awkward or uncomfortable conversation about your struggling relationship.

So what? You're not ready...

You will always regret never taking the chance, never sharing your heart, and never being truthful with the person you promised to love. But you'll never regret taking difficult action, being open and honest, and giving it your best.

You're never ready. And it always sucks.

Do it anyway. Do the difficult thing anyway.

STEP SEVEN: EMOTIONAL POWER AND MATURITY

"Your emotions are the slaves to your thoughts, and you are the slave to your emotions."
– Elizabeth Gilbert

Our young men are taught at a very young age that *boys don't cry* or they are told to *suck it up and be a man.* What that teaches those young boys is that to feel emotion isn't manly. So they stuff down emotions and put on a brave face. Those young boys turn into grown men and no one has ever taught them any differently. Today, the only real emotions we give men access to – without making it mean something derogatory about their masculinity – are anger, rage, blame, and jealousy – some of the most destructive emotions flowing in our relationships today.

As young girls we are generally more free to express emotion than boys. But as we grow a little older, we indirectly learn that our emotions make others uncomfortable. It doesn't matter if it's sadness and tears or anger and yelling. It's why at some point, someone (typically a man) has said to you, "You're so emotional," and they meant it in a derogatory way.

For all these reasons and likely many more, we suppress emotions. In our culture, we have placed a far greater value on our intellect than our emotions. But our emotions are powerful indicators for our lives. We're not terribly aware of what we're thinking moment-to-moment, but when we start to feel bad emotionally, we know it. It's actually at those first indicators of feeling really badly that we should take notice of the thoughts we're thinking that are causing those feelings, so that we can change it before any momentum gets going or any actions are taken. If we shut ourselves off to our emotions, we're only left with our intellect and, by now, you know that the mind is the thing that will lead us astray time and again from where it is we want to be. When we shut down to our emotions, we're moving through life with essentially one hand tied behind our backs.

I want to give you some context for your emotions to help you understand them so that maybe you'll begin to see them as friend rather than foe. This is an adaptation from one of my greatest teachers, Abraham-Hicks. It's called the Emotional Ladder.

The Emotional Ladder

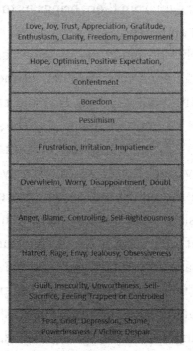

Love, Joy, Trust, Appreciation, Gratitude, Enthusiasm, Clarity, Freedom, Empowerment

Hope, Optimism, Positive Expectation,

Contentment

Boredom

Pessimism

Frustration, Irritation, Impatience

Overwhelm, Worry, Disappointment, Doubt

Anger, Blame, Controlling, Self-Righteousness

Hatred, Rage, Envy, Jealousy, Obsessiveness

Guilt, Insecurity, Unworthiness, Self-Sacrifice, Feeling Trapped or Controlled

Fear, Grief, Depression, Shame, Powerlessness / Victim, Despair

At the very bottom of the ladder are our worst feeling emotions, such as fear, grief, despair, powerlessness, and shame. Those are the nasty emotions that cause us to take to our beds in the fetal position. We're not able to make big moves from that place.

From there, the feelings of guilt, insecurity, unworthiness, or feeling trapped or controlled don't feel good either, but there's slightly more relief there than in the realm of fear, despair, depression, and shame.

One rung up from there brings us to emotions like hatred and rage.

Similarly, the emotions of anger and blame feel like a softened version of hatred and rage.

I will argue all day long that the emotion of anger is not an emotion that needs to be squelched for others to feel more comfortable. Instead, it is a productive emotion if we know how to use it. If we're in the fetal position because of despair or depression, we cannot make any big moves. However, if we're in a place of anger and blame, we can make big moves and communicate big feelings. It will be uncomfortable, but productive because you're finally telling the truth about how you feel. Anger shouldn't be squelched, it should be encouraged (although we certainly don't want to live in that space forever).

Each rung up on the ladder provides us a bit of relief. We can keep going until we reach the highest levels and the best feeling emotions of happiness, joy, appreciation, love, and empowerment.

Just having some context to where emotions exist in comparison to other emotions is helpful to understand.

- Because we're not terribly familiar with our emotions, this context allows us to identify and name what we're feeling
- This shows us why we're capable of action at certain steps and inaction at other emotional feeling states

When I want to reach for a better feeling emotion from where I am, because of this ladder, I actually know what emotion it is I'm reaching for. I might be feeling overwhelm about all the things I have to get done, but with a few minutes of effort, I could probably talk my way into feeling more of a general frustration of having to do so many things which will provide me a little bit of emotional relief and I will feel a little bit better.

And because I know that our emotions are driving our actions, I can easily see where other people are on the emotional ladder as well based upon their actions. For example, one of my clients felt like she was always getting blamed by her husband when things weren't going well in his life or in their home. I shared the emotional ladder with her and explained how blame feels so much better than guilt or insecurity. I had a hunch that her husband actually felt a lot of guilt, insecurity, and maybe even a little victimization and shame in his life, but he couldn't allow himself to feel those emotions, so instead he reached for blame. That doesn't mean his blame is accurately placed, or that she now has to pick up that blame and carry it. But it shows her that her husband is like most people, and blame just feels better than the shame. Now she at least understands why he does that repeatedly and doesn't have to get so upset about it. She knows that his blame only has the meaning she gives it and because she also knows to stay in her business, she doesn't give it much life.

Avoiding Negative Emotion

You now know something that most people of the world don't know. You know that it is our thoughts that are causing our emotions. Most people think their emotions are being driven from a circumstance. When something good happens, they feel good. When something bad happens, they feel some version of bad. You can live this way. Lots of people do. But it's a very difficult way to live because you end up feeling like a feather in a windstorm getting batted about.

We've never gotten comfortable feeling our emotions, certainly not the negative ones. No one has ever taught us how to process our emotions, so instead what we've learned is to stuff these emotions down and pretend they're not there. But when we do that, they don't go away. They actually stay with us for years or even decades, sort of like an undercurrent in our lives moving just below the surface. They're still driving our actions, we're just not consciously aware of it.

Let's be honest: negative emotions feel horrible. I'm not going to sugarcoat that for you. I don't like them any more than you do. But when we become so uncomfortable with negative emotion that it becomes scary, we run from it. Running from negative emotion looks like drinking, drugs, overeating, overworking, gambling, overspending, or even just numbing out on social media for hours on end. They don't call unhealthy food comfort food for no reason. We're using food to comfort or calm the negative emotion that we don't want to feel, so we keep eating, or drinking, or whatever until we feel numb or the absence of emotion. We do that because numb feels better than negative emotions such as fear or powerlessness.

I think we also do this because when we're feeling negative emotion, there's an underlying thought that something has gone horribly wrong. We think that the whole of life should feel good so when we don't feel good, something is wrong. But not everything in the experience of life will feel good. We hurt and struggle. We watch others hurt and struggle. We get sick. People we love become sick. There's loss. There's tragedy. There's fear, failure, and despair. But nothing has actually gone wrong.

There are those in the coaching industry that believe half of life is filled with negative emotion. I don't think that's true. Or at least, I don't think that has to be true once you learn and apply these principles. I think life can be 70-75% filled with positive emotions, such as happy and joyful, while 25-30% will create negative feeling emotions, such as sadness and anger. Even though I'm a Master Life Coach and live and breathe these teachings for a living does not mean the entirety of my life is unicorns and rainbows (or gratitude and appreciation).

Nowhere does it say our lives should be 100% positive, yet we don't teach and equip people to manage and feel their negative emotion when it arrives at their doorstep. We then create even more pain in an effort to numb or run from these emotions: sickness, alcoholism, depression, drug use, and sadly even suicide.

We indulge all these detrimental behaviors so that we don't have to feel. We're so afraid to feel. But here's what I can tell you, for certain: There's never been an emotion that killed anyone ever. An emotion, in and of itself, is harmless. It's not fun, it feels like ass, but it's not life-threatening either. Negative emotion is a part of everyone's life. No one gets out unscathed. Nothing has gone wrong. This is actually part of the contrasting life experiences that our souls signed-up for when we came into this life. Difficulties and negative emotions are going to be there, and it's going to continue driving our actions, so we need to allow negative emotion to be present without allowing it to send us down a pit from which we can never escape.

We have a choice with our negative emotions: We can stuff them down, pretend they're not there (lie to ourselves and others), and carry them with us for years or even decades. Or, alternatively, we could feel the negative emotion, process it, and then release it.

Feeling Negative Emotions

So maybe you're with me that it's better, and certainly far less destructive, to simply feel our negative emotions. And maybe you've even seen how you've run from your negative feelings in various ways. But you might be wondering, how? How do we just feel our negative emotions like fear, anger, resentment, guilt, or sadness? Here's my best recommendation and the practice that I use personally:

Let's say I wake up feeling sad. I may or may not have any reason for it. Sometimes, the circumstances in my life and my thoughts about those circumstances make me feel sad (watching my mother move through Alzheimer's or seeing my father feeling helpless in caring for her can do that to me occasionally). Sometimes it's a Tuesday and I'm sad for no good reason.

I will find a quiet place where I can sit by myself in pure silence (if you can't do that in your home, get out into nature). I set the timer on my phone for fifteen-twenty minutes. And then I invite it in: "Well, sadness, you're here so you must have something to share with me. I'm listening." And then I sit there quietly in stillness with my eyes closed and my hands palms up in my lap to welcome it in. I pay attention to my breathing and when my mind wanders, I gently guide it back to my breathing. Inevitably, it will come to the surface, maybe bringing me an ache in my chest and tears in my eyes. It might morph into something more like anger that makes my whole body tense and want to fight or run away. And sometimes, although not always, I get the message of why it's there and what it has to teach me.

When the alarm on my phone goes off, I move on with my day. I allow myself to feel the negative emotion, without drowning in it. I think oftentimes we won't allow ourselves to feel it because we're afraid it will overtake us, but it doesn't have to. Give it some space to allow it to be there, but don't give it the wheel and allow it to take over the rest of the day, the week, the month, or your life. We can feel it, giving it space in our awareness without being consumed by it.

One of my clients lived in Singapore, and her Australian husband had recently left her and her two children for another woman. My client, as you can imagine, was devastated. I shared with her this practice of allowing herself to feel all the sadness, loss, and heartbreak she was carrying. She did it. She cried her eyes out, raged, and threw some things around, fell into a small pile of pain on the floor. It lasted one hour. It felt horrible and she was so exhausted afterwards that she slept for twelve hours straight. But then, when she awakened after processing the emotion and giving herself permission to feel it, she was calmer. She told me she knew that somehow they would all be okay. She didn't feel great, but she felt some much-deserved peace.

If a woman in deep emotional pain and heartache can feel her feelings and have them pass after an hour or so, we can feel something for fifteen or twenty minutes without it pulling us under permanently.

Anything we push against only pushes back harder. There is no fight if there's nothing to push against. That's why when we resist our emotions, they actually stay with us. But when we allow the negative emotions to be there without any judgement or shame, they dissipate quickly. Give your negative emotion a space to be there without

judgement, allow it to teach you something, and then move on. It's kind of a ninja move. Give it a try.

No Such Thing as a Bad Emotion

Contrary to what you've been taught, no emotion is bad. Even the emotions of anger and blame are not bad emotions. They don't feel great, for sure, and it's not like you want to set up camp and live there, but even anger and blame feel like a breath of fresh air compared to feeling trapped or unworthy, fear and despair.

Emotions such as anger can actually serve us. Anger is sort of like jet fuel and it motivates us to take action, whereas when we're in depression and despair, all we want is our jammies, our bed, a decent movie, and maybe a bottle of wine and some ice cream. No one's taking much action from the fetal position of despair.

This is why most couples make the decision to walk out and leave their marriages after a big blow-up argument. We can take action when we're pissed off. We can walk out that door in a little self-righteous anger and slam it behind us, never looking back.

On the other end of the spectrum, the reason abused women stay in abusive relationships is because emotionally they're in some form of that fetal position at the bottom of the ladder, feeling trapped, controlled, powerless, and likely more than a little unworthy. They stay because they're paralyzed emotionally. In that example, a little anger could be helpful.

Be the Woman Who Wants to Feel

Sadness isn't exactly a fun emotion to feel. Given the choice, any of us would choose joy over sadness at every opportunity. But negative things are going to happen in this life: people we love will pass on, children will get hurt, natural disasters or wars will tear apart people's lives, and sometimes, relationships will end. I don't want to be the woman that doesn't feel any of that. When sad things happen, I'm not just willing to feel the sadness, I want to feel the sadness. And then I want to be the woman that can show up for the people I love inside of that sadness. I don't want to just be the person who's there in the good times; I want to be the person who's there through all of it. That's the woman I want to be in my relationships.

I don't want to be a stoic brick wall of a human being that never feels anything. If I was, honestly, you should worry about me. There was a teaching

I learned years ago from Dr. Brené Brown, a brilliant research professor, author, and speaker. (If you don't know who she is, seriously, look her up because she's amazing.) One of the many things I learned through her work is that we don't get to isolate what we feel. We don't get to feel all the good stuff on the top of the emotional ladder, but bypass all the negative feeling at the bottom of the ladder. We don't get to selectively feel. If we refuse to feel the lowest, most dreadful emotions, then we are also choosing to never feel the highest, most empowering, and joyful emotions. We can choose – and I think many people do choose – to remain right in the middle of that ladder, refusing to feel too many negative feelings and therefore, never having the opportunity to experience any of the really positive and joyful feelings in their life. It's like a dull pain that we become accustomed to and then we look to pharmaceuticals to help it feel a bit better.

Maybe you know someone who simply never seems really happy. Sure, there are days they're content, but for the most part they live and breathe in the space between tolerable pessimism and worrisome doubting. I actually know many of these people; I'm related to some of them. It's a dreadful way to live. It's also unnecessary. The alternative is to allow ourselves to feel the full range of our emotions. We could allow – even welcome – the most difficult emotions, so that we can also have the experience of the most invigorating and loving emotions.

Why Affirmations Don't Work

I'm clearly a fan of thinking on purpose and managing our minds so that we can feel as good as we can feel moving through this life. I'm also a fan of being aware of how we speak to ourselves, because both words and focused attention have a great deal of power. However, this is where the practice of affirmations falls down for most people.

You see, just saying you're doing great when you're actually feeling something closer to depression doesn't make it true. It actually means you're lying to yourself and the people around you, so that's not helpful.

The reason why it doesn't work is because we use things like affirmations, but we reach too far with them. We try to go from the bottom rung of the emotional ladder to the top rung of what is the equivalent of a thirty foot ladder leaned against the side of a building. Unless you're Spider-Man, that's not happening. The rest of us mere mortals have to take it one step at a time, one rung at a time. We can reach for what is one rung up from where we are currently. We cannot go from the bottom to the top in one step.

You can feel better. You can for sure reach for a better feeling thought so that you can shift the emotions you're feeling. Just do it one rung at a time and once you feel steady and stable at that rung, then you can reach for the next step. Those types of affirmative steps and self-talking exercises will get you anywhere you want to be, in virtually any circumstance.

Emotions and My Relationship?

This was a deep dive into your emotions and how powerful they truly are in your life – and your relationship. Remember, your actions have been an outcome of your emotions. And your emotions have been a result of your thoughts. So, when you can manage your mind and feel emotionally stronger, you show up differently inside of your relationship. I show up very differently when I'm in anger and blame than when I'm in irritation and impatience. And you will show up very differently when you're in overwhelm or pessimism compared to when you're feeling hopeful and optimistic. Your words change. Your energy changes. Your actions change. How you feel about your partner changes. How you engage with your partner changes.

And that changes everything.

STEP EIGHT:
INTIMACY AND CONNECTION

"Real magic in relationships means an absence of judgement of others."
– Wayne Dyer

If I walked up to any random person on the street and asked them for the definition of intimacy, my bet is most people would refer to intimacy as sex. And certainly sex can be an expression of intimacy, but intimacy, in and of itself, is a closeness and a connection between two people intellectually, physically, and emotionally.

It's a closeness that is almost palpable between two people. It's not something that you can purchase off the rack at Nordstrom's or download from Amazon. It's not something you can force or make happen. Intimacy is something that needs cultivating over time, continuously proving to one another that no matter what the other does or expresses, they are safe and loved and accepted.

Intellectual intimacy is being able to talk to one another and share ideas with one another. It's mental stimulation.

Emotional intimacy is a feeling of being deeply known by another human being and being able to deeply see, hear, and totally accept and trust them as well. It is a feeling that occurs through consistent action, but the actions themselves don't automatically lead to emotional intimacy.

Physical intimacy isn't only sex, but it is being able to express ourselves with one another sexually. It is also not only affection, but a physical comfort and closeness that includes the power of physical touch.

When one of these types of intimacy gains traction in our relationship it can create opportunity for others to take root and grow as well. To have all three is achieving the intimacy trifecta, which is an admirable goal for sure, but difficult to attain simultaneously. Know that these will each ebb and flow at different times of your relationship and that's completely normal. Intimacy isn't like a degree that you achieve once and then you can hang it on your wall forever.

The psychologist Deborah Leupnitz wrote a book titled *Schopenhauer's Porcupines*. In it, she uses the porcupine metaphor to demonstrate how intimacy with humans is much like porcupines on a cold winter night. To keep from freezing, they huddle close together. But as soon as they get close enough to truly warm one another, they get poked by each other's quills and are forced to separate. So, they go between getting cold, moving closer, and being close to one another, but causing themselves pain. Hence, the dilemma in creating intimacy.

Intimacy Is Only an Issue in Our Long-Term Relationships

Intimacy is created where both openness and acceptance are present. When we are free to be completely open with our partners knowing that we will be accepted and loved no matter what is expressed (even when it's not glamorous or pretty), intimacy has fertile ground to grow.

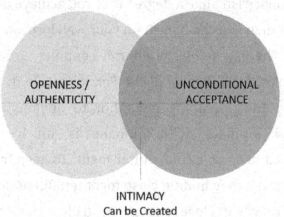

OPENNESS /
AUTHENTICITY

UNCONDITIONAL
ACCEPTANCE

INTIMACY
Can be Created

Also, it's worth saying that for intimacy to take root between a couple that openness and unconditional acceptance needs to go both ways. If one person holds back because they don't feel emotionally safe, then the other partner is going to feel that distance and won't be open and authentic to create true intimacy.

Intimacy was never an issue that we needed to think about before getting into long-term committed relationships. When you're only with someone for a short time, everything feels new and interesting as you're learning about one another. Even when you've been together for a few years, remaining close feels effortless as long as trust exists between the partners. To maintain an intimate relationship over the course of decades, we are constantly navigating knowing and honoring who we are as individuals and knowing and honoring who we are as part of a couple.

Knowing and Honoring Ourselves

If we are going to open ourselves up in an intimate relationship with another human being, we need to know who we truly are and like that person looking in the mirror. Without that awareness and self-acceptance, we inevitably hide parts of ourselves that we don't fully accept and therefore, don't want to share with another.

In my opinion, this is one of the greatest deterrents to intimacy in our relationships today.

All of us carry with us wounds from our lives. Life can be heartbreakingly difficult at times and no one goes unscathed. Those experiences can leave us with wounds that impact how we feel about ourselves and those are the very things that we want to suppress from ourselves and hide from others. Whenever we hide parts of ourselves, it limits our ability to really be free to be open in our most intimate relationships.

If we're both wearing a mask of some sort, how are we ever truly supposed to really know one another?

If we don't love and accept ourselves, why in the world should we expect someone else to fully love and accept us?

This is why personal growth work is really foundational to being able to create and sustain healthy, loving, connected relationships.

As we become more aware and accepting of ourselves, it changes the way we show up in our relationships.

I had a client that I'll refer to as Margaret, who was such a sweet, kind, gentle, and loving soul. Margaret was married to an investment advisor for thirty-three years, and although she had a real estate career of her own, that career always took the backseat to her husband, her family, and her home life. She and her husband got along well enough, but they were no longer operating as a couple together, not having had sex in years and with her feeling alone and unsupported. She had recently discovered that her husband had been having an affair with someone he worked with and this absolutely crushed her self-esteem.

We began working together, intentionally taking the focus off her husband and the effort to fix the relationship for a moment. Often stepping away from the very thing we most want to fix is the only way to gain the necessary perspective to create the real change we desire. After all, she had been attempting to wrestle it to the ground by knowing where he was and what he was doing at all times (controlling his behavior so she felt safer) and that hadn't worked yet so it was time to attempt a different approach. I wanted to place the focus back on her, so she could begin to see herself through new eyes. If she wanted to remain in her marriage, I wanted her to do that from a place of confidence, rather than insecurity.

From this new vantage point, Margaret discovered:

- As she began to truly know and appreciate the love she had to give in the relationship, her husband also began to notice and appreciate her more. Once she was no longer begging him to stay, and instead encouraging him to get clear about what he really wanted and whether or not he wanted to be there with her from a place of confidence, he was no longer resisting the marriage. Instead, he was trying to convince her why she should give him another chance.

- The more and more that she began to know who she was in the relationship, the higher the bar raised for her husband and their relationship, and, believe it or not, he was taking the steps to meet her there at this new place

Time will tell if the relationship between Margaret and her husband can be healed. He's trying in a new way and she's allowing herself to feel her emotions, while holding very clear boundaries. In all my years coaching women through deep pain and heartbreak, I have never seen a woman like Margaret. She has become such a strong and confident woman in the face of incredibly difficult circumstances, while still maintaining her tenderness and ability to forgive. If anyone can move on from that, I promise you it is Margaret and by applying these same tools I've shared in this book, she will be happy and whole, regardless of whether or not the relationship finds that same soft landing place.

We bring all that we are – and all that we believe is possible for ourselves – into our most intimate relationships. When we change how we show up in these relationships, we automatically create change in our relationships. When we change what we desire and know what we truly deserve, we change the dynamics within the relationship itself.

When we expand what we believe is possible, new opportunities for connection also arise.

Knowing and Honoring Who We Are as a Couple

I learned the most about how to honor who we are inside of our relationships from the book *The Zimzum of Love* by Rob Bell, who co-authored the book with his wife, Kristen Bell. In this book, they introduce the idea that the space between you and your spouse – the space that is your relationship itself – exists nowhere else on the planet and should be treated as special...even sacred.

For that reason, you don't invite others into that space. Inviting others in includes:

- Talking to family or friends about the struggles you're experiencing in your marriage
- Speaking disrespectfully about your spouse to others
- Not having your partner's back when someone else speaks disrespectfully about them
- Certainly, this also includes both emotional and physical affairs

We've probably all spoken about the issues within our marriages to others at some point.

We're not intending to disrespect the relationship. Sometimes we're wanting another opinion from someone who isn't emotionally involved and sometimes we're simply trying to make sure we're not crazy. But oftentimes, there's an element of needing to feel right and justified in how we feel, and we think there's strength and confidence to be gained when others agree with us. No one else needs to justify your experience for it to be real and true for you. And when we share intimate pieces of ourselves or pieces of the relationship with others, it disrespects the relationship itself.

Inside of a couple, private things are shared between two souls: goals and aspirations, doubts and fears, challenges and insecurities, desires, and dreams. There are some things that need to remain private between the two of you. That doesn't mean you can never talk to anyone, but I promise it will be more productive for you to speak with a professional to obtain an unbiased opinion than a close confidant.

When you share the details of your relationship with others (even those who you love and love you) you are inviting them into a place where they don't belong. Your family and friends do not belong in the middle of your marriage. And when you share details with them, you're rolling out the red carpet for them to have an opinion. They're going to tell you their opinion, what they think you should do, based upon your perspective you've shared and how that gets interpreted through their own lens. Embedded in that opinion will be their fears, judgements, and beliefs. Plus those people who love you want to support you and certainly don't want to see you hurting, so the advice they give you will be through that particular lens. But this is not theirs to do, it is not their decision. It is yours and right now you don't need more voices to add to the clutter in your mind and your heart. You actually need less noise, less clutter, more clarity.

Plus, we've all been in that awkward situation where we've made our partners out to the villain with our family and friends and then after we've made peace with it, the family and friends are still struggling with what you told them previously.

After speaking to thousands of people about their relationships, there is one thing I know for certain: No one truly knows what's happening in a relationship that they're not intimately involved in themselves. I can speak to a woman struggling in her marriage and she will give me her perspective. Then I could speak to her husband and he will have a completely different perspective. So if the two people that live and breathe in that relationship every single day do not see it the same way, how in the world can anyone outside the relationship truly understand what's going on?

Other people agreeing with you might make you feel better in the moment (so you can be right or righteous), but it will only create more confusion and new problems to overcome, should you attempt to repair the relationship in the future.

Creating and Deepening Connection

We've all read a book or seen some therapist that tells you to have a "date night" once a week. That's fine, except when we spend most of it is in silence because we forgot how to talk to one another, only placing a spotlight on the very thing we don't do well right now, which is communicating.

I'm sure some well-meaning person along the way has told you to ride it out and that eventually the storm will pass. The problem is the storm not only hasn't magically passed, it's worsened over time and now it feels like either a never-ending drought (leaving you feeling empty and alone) or a perpetual hurricane (leaving nothing but destruction in its wake).

You've probably been to a counselor or expert who told you to touch one another, to hold hands or look one another in the eyes, which sounds great except that because you're struggling right now it just feels forced and awkward as hell.

I think the single most underutilized means of creating connection between two people is to become curious again about one another.

A long time ago I read a quote – I cannot remember who said it and I've searched for it endlessly so I know these aren't the exact words, but here it goes: "The moment you stop being curious about a woman is the moment you begin to lose her."

Even though you've been together for decades.

Even though you feel like you've talked about everything.

Even though you feel like you know everything there is to know about your partner.

There is nothing on this planet that does not change: the blades of grass, the leaves on the trees, the car you drive each day, the cells in your body. There is nothing that is not changing in every moment. So what in the world makes us think that our partners will never change from the day we marry them? Neither of us are frozen in time on the day we marry.

That's impossible.

Everyone is changing and as their partners we're either resisting that change or celebrating it. When we give up our expectations of what we expect them to be, we have the potential to love and celebrate each new version of themselves that they become.

My clients are often women in their forties and fifties. Their kids are (nearly) grown and there's finally space in their lives for themselves again. They begin exploring new interests, many want to travel, or move their bodies in new ways through dance or yoga. And after giving so many years to everyone else's needs, they don't make any apologies for wanting to pursue things that interest them.

I often hear about the husbands of those clients lamenting about the changes they see in their wives. They tell her things like, "You've changed. I don't even know who you are anymore. You're so selfish now." Change is difficult for people, but it gives us the choice to either resist that change and need it to be different so we can feel better or safer, or we can become curious about who our partners are becoming. Not all change is bad. Most change is good, because it's new, improved evolution of what existed previously. That new iPhone in your pocket is probably lightyears better than the cell phone you carried ten years ago, but none of us resisted that change. I never knew I needed heated seats in my car until I had them. We embrace the next version of all the tools and technologies around us, but for some reason we resist it when people change and evolve.

You're changing each and every moment as a result of your experience in this life.

And so is your partner.

Get curious again. Assume there are things you do not know about your partner.

Maybe you stopped talking to him about the things that interest and inspire you because he's not interested in those same things.

Maybe he stopped talking to you about the things that interested and motivated him because you're not interested in those same things.

So that leaves us with the common ground of things like....well, the weather and the news.

Ugh.

When we stop being curious about our partners our relationship slowly begins to die.

Certainly when all we talk about is the kids, the weather, and the news – it's time to pay attention and make some changes.

My husband loves to talk about health, nutrition, and how the body works. He literally would do it for hours on end if he could. That's not really my thing. Instead, I would love nothing more than to talk about relationships and human behavior until the wee hours of the morning. But that's not really his thing. It doesn't matter that health and nutrition isn't my favorite topic. I want to hear about it because he's interested in it and I am interested in him. It doesn't really matter that relationships and human behavior aren't his favorite topics because he knows it's important to me. When you're interested in and genuinely curious about your partner, you want to hear about the things that are capturing their attention.

Even if it's not a topic that you're deeply interested in, listen anyway so that you can know your partner a little more deeply and he can feel heard and understood.

Don't hold back on sharing a new idea you thought of or a dream that's been calling to you lately. Don't keep the best moments of your day to yourself. Joy is multiplied when it's shared. Your partner may or may not be interested in that topic personally. If he's interested in you, he'll want to hear what interests and excites you.

That's what keeps us actively and intellectually engaged with one another.

That's where we feel known, heard, and understood.

That's what keeps us connected as we move and grow through life together.

Curiosity in Action

There was an exercise in the book The Normal Bar that will likely help you learn something new about your spouse and can provide an opportunity for connection:

1. Create a list of five things that you need to be happy in life, but none of those things can have anything to do with the spouse or the kids

2. Share the list with your partner. The spouse that's not sharing has to listen, without debating or criticizing. After all, an individual's preferences are being expressed, so there is no right or wrong answer.

3. Identify what you know now that you didn't know previously, either about yourself, or your partner.

I did this exercise with my husband, Derrick.

My five things were:

1. Friendships
2. Yoga

3. Continuous learning and personal/spiritual growth

4. Puppies (Leo & Luna)

5. Sunshine/warm weather

His five things were:

1. God

2. Health

3. Good sleep

4. Succeeding in his business and being his own boss

5. Warm weather (all year round)

I surprised him because he thought my list would closely mirror his. Like many of us, he assumed that I wanted the same things he wanted, but outside of sunshine and warm weather, our lists were entirely different. He surprised me by how important it is for him to succeed in a new business that he's creating. I didn't realize it would rank in his top five needs for happiness. That's really good for me to know so that I can be supportive of him as he expands professionally.

Consider giving it a try with your spouse.

Sometimes creating those subtle shifts has far more to do with how we're being, rather than what we're doing. Maybe it's just a matter of becoming curious about your partner again and finding the connection points between you.

You Cannot Force Intimacy

One of my clients was this amazing entrepreneur, who I'll call Amanda. She had been married to her husband for twelve years and they had two kids together. She and her husband never really had a great sex life, but over the course of the last five years, it had become almost non-existent. She went to bed naked almost every night, she made attempts to be physical with him, but she was literally rejected again and again. After a while she simply gave up trying.

And as you can imagine, that took its toll on the marriage. They became about the business of running their businesses, raising the kids, and renovating a home together. Fast forward to a few years later and even though she never intended it or saw it coming, Amanda fell in love with someone else.

Now the marriage wasn't just sexless and disconnected, it was in crisis and her husband was paying attention. Because he knew that sex was important to her all those years ago, he wanted to solve the problems in their marriage by having sex every other day. But, now it was just awkward and felt really forced for Amanda. Plus, she now knew what real connection, closeness, and intimacy felt like. Once you know that, you cannot un-know it and pretend it doesn't exist. There was no going back to being the woman who has given up on having true intimacy – both physical and emotional intimacy. She was no longer willing to live without that and it wasn't just about sex. Now she wanted something much deeper.

I know we've been taught that when there's a challenge in our lives that we need to get into action mode and fix it. But I would argue that's actually the worst thing you can do when it comes to creating connection and intimacy.

Amanda's husband thought sex was the answer, so he quickly got a prescription for erectile dysfunction. But that felt false to Amanda. That didn't mean he desired her. It just meant he wanted to have sex with anything once he took a pill.

Intimacy is about creating connection and closeness and for that to happen, we need to feel safe emotionally. If it feels awkward or forced, it's not going to be effective. Rather than attempting to wrestle the problems to the ground and work hard to figure out a solution, we need more allowing, more openness, more acceptance, more curiosity, and yes, more communication.

Nurturing Your Own Energy

This may sound a little off-topic from intimacy, but it's not. To have a truly intimate relationship with someone, you have to nurture your sexual, sensual, and feminine energies, allowing yourself to be fully seen by your partner. If you are from a similar generation as me, then you very likely were never taught about your sexuality, sensuality, and femininity. And if you grew up in "the church," like me, you likely not only didn't talk about those things, but there might have been some shame in ever even acknowledging their presence. Hence one of the many reasons we struggle with intimacy. We live in a society where passion (in all its forms) is judged or frowned upon, which has disconnected us from our bodies and our feelings. That's not done us any favors in the intimacy department.

Your sexual, sensual, and feminine energies reside in the sacral energy center. If you're not familiar with the chakras, they're just another way to look at the human body. I learned from Dr. Deepak Chopra, M.D. that in the Western world, we look at the body through the lens of anatomy: essentially tissues, blood, and bones. In the Eastern world, the map they use of the body is more about the meridians and the flow of energy through the body, knowing that all pieces of the body are connected. And in India, the map they use for the human body is energy centers known as chakras.

That helped me to see that no one perspective is right or wrong, it's just different ways to see the same human body. The sacral chakra – where these sexual, sensual, and feminine energies reside – exists between the base of the spine and the navel. The sacral chakra is our pleasure and energy center. The gift of this chakra is experiencing our lives through pleasure, feelings, and sensations. It is also the center of feeling, emotion, pleasure, sensuality, intimacy, and connection.

Here's why this is important. Passion is the fuel behind all creative energy. Everything we create – a poem, a photograph, a home, a business, even a child – originates from the energy of the sacral chakra.

Sexual Energy is about being fully present in your body and owning every piece of it as you are. We've all known people who may not have been the perfect size six, but who totally owned and lived in their bodies. It's almost palpable and we're drawn to that energy. Most of us as women struggle with this. We're so hard on our bodies because we've been taught how we should look (from advertising, culture, society, etc.), rather than embracing how we *actually do* look. Sexual energy is all about going beyond self-acceptance and really loving our physical selves.

When we're hiding because we don't like or accept our bodies, we don't allow our partners to really see us.

When we're hiding, we create walls around us and tell ourselves it's for our own protection. But those walls create distance between us and others...and loneliness.

If we don't love ourselves unconditionally, how can we possibly expect others to do for us what we're not willing to do for ourselves?

This is why sexual energy is such an important component to creating intimacy.

Sensual Energy is when you are fully present with another person. When we simply stop and focus 100% of our attention on the person we're with, we're allowing ourselves to be fully seen and we're fully seeing the other person as well. What a gift that presence is to someone you love. Presence has become a rare gift during a time when we are constantly connected and overstimulated through technology (hence the reason to put your phone down). When you are fully present with someone, it's fertile ground for intimacy to be created. It's fertile ground for closeness to be cultivated. Sensual energy isn't about your output, efficiency, or your to-do list. It's about your presence in the moment with another soul.

Feminine Energy is our ability to soften. To soften our energy is to breathe and relax into a knowing that all is well, even if circumstances might indicate otherwise. There's nothing to force or push to make happen. Instead, we can trust in something beyond ourselves. We can even trust in the things we categorize as miraculous:

We can trust that our blood is pumping all on its own and that our lungs are breathing and it's not on our to-do lists.

We can trust that we are being held, guided, and absolutely adored by the same energy that raises the sun every morning and places the stars in the sky each evening.

We can trust in the energy of love. We can freely love others and allow ourselves to be loved, knowing that love is our true nature and that's why it feels most like home.

For some of us, we barely know what that word, soften, means. I know first-hand how it felt to "armor up" every day before going into work when I was a corporate executive. There was no room for softness in that life. I felt that any success, security, or achievement was only going to happen if I made it happen through sheer will. So to feel successful of course I tried to control my very controllable husband and the circumstances in our lives. I pushed hard on so many fronts and then I brought that same energy home with me at night into my marriage (that must have been fun to curl up next to at night).

As women, we've had to put up so many brick walls around us that we quietly believe if we soften into a relationship (or fully and completely trust a man), it means we're weak in some way, which we have railed against for at least a century to still find our place where we are today.

The very thing that has served so many of us Type A women (strong, successful, driven, ambitious, busy) might be the very thing that prevents us from having intimacy in our marriages. It might be the very thing that makes us hesitate to allow ourselves to be held, seen, and fully experienced by our beloveds. Although our independence can be a superpower in some regard, it can also be our kryptonite.

Masculine energy, in comparison, is more of a push yourself, decisive, and get-it-done approach to life. We all have both masculine and feminine energies within us, but sometimes one type is more dominant. Because I can bring masculine energy with very little effort, I have to make an effort to nurture my feminine energy and give it permission to flow. That might look like wearing soft, silky fabrics only because they feel good against my skin. That might look like dancing and moving my body. It might be giving in to let my husband take care of and hold me, without it taking away any of my power as a woman.

I've come to think of it as a dial that I have control over. Sometimes I genuinely need to bring more masculine energy to what is happening in my life, while other times what I need is to soften and allow what wants to happen to take place (releasing the need to attempt to control). I can intentionally dial one up and deliberately dial the other down, being conscious about when each serves me best. If I'm training for a marathon or needing to bring a project across the finish line, I need more of my masculine energy. But when it comes to being present with my beloved or creating from inspiration, I need more of my feminine energy to be present. We have all the control once we realize when to use what type of energy in our relationships.

Our sexual, sensual, and feminine energies allow us to be fully seen, help us to be fully present, and give us the opportunity to soften in our most intimate relationships. When we resist those energies, we rarely feel close or truly connected to our partners, which limits intimacy. And often, we blame him for that. However, when we consciously and intentionally nurture these energies, we're able to be present in our bodies, present with our partners, and simultaneously both strong and soft within the relationship. And on any given day, that can feel like a miracle.

STEP NINE:
THE DECISION

"I trust the next chapter because I know the author."
– Unknown Author

I love the idea of having someone to walk beside in this life.

I love that we get to be a witness to one another's lives.

I love that we get to share the joys and sorrows of life with another human being.

And, yet, the institution of marriage is sort of a peculiar thing to me.

Marriage was originally created as an alliance between two families, where the property rights, money, and bloodlines could be secured within the family. It also was a way to expand the family's labor force through women and to combine assets for more power.

The notion of marriage becoming a religious sacrament can be traced back to St. Paul as a means of keeping people from being sinful and procreating outside of the family.

Not to be left out, states began playing a bigger role in the definition of marriage, requiring marriage licenses in 1639.

Even today, the vow "...Until death do us part," is a way to keep people from divorcing. You will not leave no matter how much we hurt one another. Sounds more like prison than love.

You'll notice a consistent theme here: control.

Marriage was not about companionship or mutual attraction or even love. The history of marriage is about control and power (and a healthy dose of fear).

Mind you, this is coming from a woman that is married....happily married, as a matter of fact. But I still consciously choose my husband each and every day. I am not standing beside him out of obligation or because the government says I have to because we're legally married. I am not standing by his side as both a partner and a lover because if I left, I believe he would fall apart without me and I would feel too guilty. That's not love, that's prison. I am standing beside him because there is nowhere else on the planet I would rather be than beside that man. I chose him years ago and I still choose him each day.

In today's environment, we expect our spouses to be everything to us: our lover, our soul mate, our best friend, our confidant, our biggest fan, and our greatest supporter. We want them to be simultaneously dependable, known, and loyal, but also passionate, spontaneous, and exciting. It's a tall order that we place on our marriages. And we don't automatically get both love and passion in the same relationship without some very intentional effort.

We're also in a time where we can create anything we want – including in a relationship. But we cannot do that without evolving who we are and how we're showing up inside those relationships. The days of looking to our spouses to make us happy have expired. It's not their jobs. It's never been their jobs. And I would argue they haven't been successful at making us feel happy despite even their best efforts to do all the things we wanted them to do.

Marriage, as an institution, isn't going away anytime soon.

But I do believe that anything rooted in fear and obligation will struggle to thrive without some real evolution and consciousness brought to the relationship so that the two people in it can simultaneously choose themselves and one another again and again and again.

Making a Choice to Stay

Many of my private clients come to the end of the work we do together and consciously make the choice to remain in the relationship and to continue letting it evolve and grow.

When Natalie reached out to me she was lost and confused. She had just ended an affair she engaged in, after finding out that her husband of sixteen years had been having an affair with someone at work for the last several months. He told her that it was only talking and flirting, but she's not sure she believed him, and she didn't really have much righteousness to stand on since she had been having an affair herself. They were in a crisis, both hurt and scared, when she and I began working together. She was willing to try to make her relationship feel good again and so I equipped her with many of the tools I've outlined in this book, personally coaching her through each of them. By the end of our work together she told me that she and her husband were closer than they've been in a long time, and she felt hopeful again for their relationship and their family.

Natalie didn't have to stay. She could have left, thinking that she could be happier with someone else. But even though she had strayed, she'd not entirely given up hope on her husband and their relationship. She wanted to try again. She chose to try again. And she chose to keep trying.

Rather than staying in the marriage because you feel as though you have to, stay in the marriage because you choose to. That one mental shift can provide some breathing room for something new to be created. When you own your choices, it helps you feel empowered in your own life.

You're not stuck.

You're not confused.

You're making a conscious choice today (and you may make a different choice in the future).

We've been struggling lately, but today I choose to remain in the relationship and actively look for new ways for it to feel good again.

Today I choose my beloved. I choose to stay and keep trying to create something new together.

I'm going to give this marriage my very best effort and in the end, if it still doesn't feel good for us, we're going to make the decision to stop hurting one another and move forward in our lives.

You get to choose. So does your partner.

You wouldn't want your husband to remain in the relationship with you solely out of obligation, would you? If he only stayed because he felt trapped, would that relationship ever feel like enough for you?

The best marriages are those where, even in their turmoil, there are two people who keep showing up for one another and there's no one else they'd rather be with.

Likewise, you don't want to stay in the marriage because of the metaphorical shackles around your ankles that keep you stuck. You want to be there out of your choosing. Even in the midst of a struggle, you can choose one another. You can choose to apply what you've learned so that you continue to grow closer as a couple and find more freedom and acceptance in your love together.

When people find me, their marriage needs an answer and I don't take any choice off the table for the woman struggling in her marriage. I don't have an agenda for her life because I don't believe there is any *wrong* answer (except continuing to lie to yourself and not answering). I just don't have that judgement. My job isn't to judge my clients and attempt to push them into one specific direction of either staying no matter what or leaving no matter what. My job is to help them come to a decision within themselves that honors them and the relationship, created more from an internal knowledge than external rules. And if they genuinely want to make the marriage work again, my job is to equip them with the tools so that they can create something new together that feels good for them both. And if they know that their answer is to leave, I honor that choice as well and will equip them to unwind the relationship as peacefully and lovingly as possible.

Making a Choice to Leave

If you've genuinely applied the concepts within this book over and over again, if you've put forward your very best effort to create a new kind of relationship together and you find that the relationship is still painful for one or both of you, then you do have an answer for yourself.

It may not be a simple answer.

It may not be the answer that would make everyone else comfortable.

It may not be the answer you were hoping for. But it is an answer.

When I spoke with my client Beth for the first time, she told me she was crying every day because she didn't know how to stay in her thirty-one year marriage, but she didn't want to hurt her husband by divorcing either. Beth had married her high school sweetheart. He was the only man she'd ever loved and she had been separated from him for over a year. During that time, she realized she didn't miss him, "because he never really shared that much of himself with her." She had always known something was missing in their relationship, but they had a family together – a beautiful, amazing family and a lot of history together - so she stayed. She told me how he was smart and good looking, but also unaffectionate and distant. There were no hugs or kissing, no sweet words or "I love yous." He was controlling and had a temper, and she had learned early on to go with what he wanted as to avoid an argument and keep the peace between them.

Beth was a nurse by trade, so she had always taken care of everyone else. If she wasn't taking care of her husband, it was her kids. If it wasn't her kids, it was her patients. She was literally trained and rewarded for taking care of everyone else's needs. It didn't seem that unusual to completely subjugate her needs, desires, and preferences for decades at home as well.

She did that until she simply couldn't anymore. Her boys had grown up and left the family home, off to build happy, productive lives of their own. She was proud of them, and of herself as a mother. But she had no idea who she was as a woman.

She could not go buy something and bring it into the house without her husband agreeing to it. He had very distinct preferences. Now that she had her own place, it was filled with things that she likes, the things that bring her joy. In her marriage, she was made fun of by her husband if she would read either spiritual or self-help books, so she never did. Now, she had a bookshelf full of inspirational and spiritual teachings.

She was discovering who she was now and for the life of her – even though she loved her husband – she couldn't figure out how to go back into that marriage. It would have been so much easier. It wouldn't break-up the family. It wouldn't hurt the only man she had ever loved. But she could no longer deny her own needs, desires, and preferences (and put up with what she didn't realize was abusive behavior) inside her most intimate relationship. She was waking up.

And, as often happens, Beth attracted someone into her life now that made her feel cherished and valued. He wanted to know who she was and celebrated and adored what he found. He was affectionate and loving, open, and vulnerable. She had found the elusive space of intimacy with this man and it was very confusing to her. She was riddled with guilt, but now that she knew what that felt like, she couldn't turn away from the way it fed her soul.

Many people might judge Beth, but I don't. If you're walking through the desert with no food and water for decades and someone offers you a plate and cup of water, you're going to take it. She's literally one of the best human beings I've ever met, and she was far more judgmental of herself than she had ever been to anyone else.

She didn't leave her marriage for this other man. She left her marriage for herself. She had no idea if this new man was going to be her new "forever." She wasn't even sure there was such a thing as forever anymore. But she did know that her next thirty years could not be the same as her previous thirty years. And since she had left, her husband hadn't changed at all. Beth left her marriage and ultimately divorced from her husband, but she did so in the most intentional and peaceful way possible. They were no longer married, but because they had children and grandchildren together, they would also be in relationship with one another – just in a new way. She left with no regrets, knowing that she had tried absolutely everything she could over the last several years to make the relationship work for her before making the painful decision to end it.

What Now?

That answer, in my experience, tends to be one that comes from the quiet whispers of the soul, an internal knowing that feels like truth in the body, rather than a cerebral exercise backed up by pros and cons lists. Even though it might feel like a pit in your stomach, there's a knowing that's present within us at that moment of realization that this is the decision.

If you've made the painful decision to leave, your mind now has a problem that it wants to solve in order to keep you safe:

Where will you live? Where will he live?
You need to get an attorney.

How in the world will you tell him? What's his reaction going to be?

My best advice to you in that moment of realization is to slow down. Your mind is going to go into overdrive presenting you with every possible frightening scenario that you'll think you have to solve right now. You don't. That's just your primitive mind attempting to keep you safe in what is a frightening circumstance. Interrupt the busy mind with this thought: *There will be a time for us to figure out all the details of unwinding this marriage; now is not that time.*

It was a Monday morning when I received the text message from another client, Tracey: "I feel like I'm coming to this fork in the road in my marriage again. I want more than what he's ever been able to give to me. My gut tells me I don't want to stay in this relationship." She knew for sure that she had tried absolutely everything to make the relationship feel good again, applying all the tools she had learned repeatedly. Tracey and I had a coaching call together and, on that day, she was beginning to come to terms with her marriage being over, or rather...complete. She was now able to move forward with a clear heart, no regrets, and even loving thoughts about her husband.

When you have the realization that your marriage is over, I think that deserves some reverence before automatically jumping into action mode. Just let that settle in for a day or two or ten. Then, you can begin to wrap your mind around having that initial conversation with your husband and all that will follow that moment when you express the words, "For me, this marriage is over."

STEP TEN:
SHOWING UP IN LOVE

"We are not asking you to love THIS.
We are asking you to love."
– Abraham-Hicks

Whether you've made the decision to stay and continue working on the marriage or whether you've made the decision to leave the marriage, your next step is to show up in love.

What It Means to Show Up in Love

To love and to be loving to our partners is an action, a choice we make. But when we engage in the action of loving to receive love in return, we're starting from a place of what we can get rather than what we have to give. Relationships tend to not work very well when we're attempting to get something from someone else.

So love, of course. Take the actions of being loving toward one another, but do so because it feels good to love, not to get something in return.

Love because it's your true nature to love.

Love because it's who you are.

Love because it's all we're here to do and it's the whole point of our lives.

Society would tell you that your purpose in this life is to grow up, obey your parents, get good grades, get an education, get a job, own a home, take on debt, start a family, pay bills, be kind and loving toward those that are kind and loving toward you, try to not get too sick, and then eventually die of old age.

I would argue that your purpose is to come here into this life to love and to allow yourself to be loved, as well as to grow and allow others to grow as well. Some of those other things happen, of course, but in the midst of it, the whole point is to love and grow.

Show Up in Love Whether You Choose to Stay or Go

Showing up in love seems logical when you've made the choice to remain in the relationship. You keep tending to the garden of your relationship, applying the tools so that you're better able to communicate and grow closer and more connected over time. You manage your mind so that you're showing up in the relationship as the woman that you want to be. Make the choice to be loving even when he doesn't deserve it. Make the choice to be loving to yourself by setting healthy boundaries. Make the choice to love so that you can feel good in the relationship, lining up with your decision to stay and evolve the relationship so it feels good again.

Showing up in love when you're choosing to leave the relationship is a little less intuitive. That's because we've been taught that you must hate him as pretext for leaving the relationship. If you had love for him, then you would stay, right? After all, there's not a story written or a movie made that does not have a villain in it. So our minds go looking for the villain. And we think that either we're the bad person in this story or he is.

What if no one is wrong? What if you're both completely and totally deserving of love and understanding? What if you're both good people and the relationship itself just didn't work for one or both of you? What if the relationship wasn't supposed to last forever and now it's complete?

When you start to look at it through that lens, you truly can unwind a marriage in a loving and peaceful manner. I tell my clients that a year or so from now you will look back on this time in your life – this difficult time of walking away from a marriage – and you're going to want to be able to say, "I'm proud of how I handled that. It was not easy, but I'm proud of myself for how I showed up in the midst of that difficult circumstance." Let that goal of being able to look yourself years from now in the mirror guide you through this process. Every time it gets difficult to be loving, that thought of looking back on this time and wanting to feel good about how you handled a difficult situation will change how you react and move through this.

Just because most people don't do divorce in a loving and peaceful way doesn't mean that it's not possible. Most people don't have the tools you now have. Most people act out in hurt and anger, feeling punched they want to punch back, and what I'm inviting you to do is to put your weapons down. The fights about who was wrong and needs to change have all been had...likely hundreds of times. Now is the time to intentionally dial down the drama and get clear about what's really important to you, because not everything you will fight about will matter in a few years from now. (I had a client whose husband was battling her for the dinner plates and flatware when they divorced; I promise you will not care about the dinner plates a year from now...let him have them.)

If you're willing to walk away in love, you will:

Not have to endure months (or years) of hatefulness toward the person you once loved. (A loving act for yourself.)

Not unintentionally force your children to navigate not having Mom and Dad in the same room together at graduations, weddings, the first birthday party of your first grandchild...all because the two of you couldn't be emotional adults through this process and now despise one another. (A loving act for your children.)

Give your future ex-husband the best opportunity of finding his own happiness. You may not realize it now, but you actually do want that. If he's happy, he's not tormenting himself about you. If he's happy, he's moving on with his life. If he's the father of your children, I promise that you want him to be happy, healthy, and thriving in his life for the benefit of your children. (And that is a loving act for everyone.)

My ex-husband moved on very quickly after I left. Although it's a broad generalization, men do tend to move on quickly after a marriage ends. There are lots of philosophies on why this happens, but mostly it's because men do better personally and professionally when they're in a relationship.

I literally had a client this afternoon tell me that her husband went out on a date last week and they had only made the decision to separate less than two weeks ago. His first priority wasn't figuring out new living arrangements or how to tell the kids, it was setting up an online profile and going on a date.

But having been on the other side of that myself, what I can tell you is that it brought me a great deal of peace to think that my ex found someone that thinks he's utterly fantastic. He's not a bad person, undeserving of love. (I don't actually believe that anyone is undeserving of love.) He just wasn't my person and I wasn't his. It was long overdue that we told the truth about that.

If I know anything about love, I do know this: we all want to be loved. To have love, you need to become love. You need to become the one who loves. Not love pointed at you, but love flowing through you. And when you do that, you'll never have a shortage of it in your life. And to love and to be loved is the whole damn point.

Our Greatest Teachers

By now, you know that I have many teachers: Martha Beck, Wayne Dyer, Elizabeth Gilbert, Rob Bell, Elizabeth Lesser, Marianne Williamson, Byron Katie, and Abraham-Hicks.

If you want to know where to find the greatest spiritual teachers for your life, look no further than your closest, most intimate relationships.

Unlike traditional teachers who are there to impart wisdom, our closest relationships are there to expose all the parts of ourselves that we don't really want to see, to teach us about forgiveness and acceptance, to bring to light our beliefs about our ability to love and be loved. They are there to help us heal our wounds. Sometimes they are there to provide the necessary contrast we need in order to get really clear about what our hearts really desire.

- They will show us how our judgements of them are really just a mirror to the pieces of ourselves that we're not yet ready to own
- They will bring to light all of our underlying fears that have not yet been addressed

- They will demonstrate just how many expectations and conditions we place on our love and give us the opportunity to rethink those conditions
- Our marriages will show us how we've learned and applied the same unhealthy behaviors we saw at home growing up into our current relationships
- They will most certainly teach us about forgiveness
- These closest relationships will show us the correlation between the depth of emotional pain and the depth to which we're willing to love. And when that emotional pain brings us to our knees, it will force us to walk through it in order to get to the other side of it.
- Your relationship with your life partner will undoubtedly teach you that it is only through great honesty, trust, and vulnerability that you will ever truly find great intimacy, passion, and love.

The people in our lives that we open the deepest parts of our hearts to are there for us as both our greatest spiritual challenge and our greatest spiritual teachers. They're divine gifts to open us up to the deeper truths of who we really

are and to challenge us to become our highest and best version of ourselves. No one will challenge us the way our beloveds will, and no one will teach us more about ourselves.

CONCLUSION: THE DIFFERENCE

"If I accept the fact that my relationships are here to make me conscious, instead of happy, then my relationships become a wonderful self-mastery tool that keeps realigning me with my higher purpose for living."
– Eckhart Tolle

Some people will read this book and come to their decision – the one they will never second-guess. They will write to me and tell me how my teachings changed their lives and how grateful they are to have found me. Others will read it and reach out and tell me, "It wasn't worth the money. I've heard all this before." Same teachings, different result. How can that be? The only variable is the person consuming the information.

Why Do Some People Get Clarity and Others Stay Stuck?

Let's be real. Lots of people struggle in their marriages. Just consider that the divorce rate is 50% for first marriages and much higher for second or third marriages. That alone is a lot of people who struggle enough to call it quits. But that does not account for all the people who stay married but are miserable, frustrated, feeling empty, and stuck. They don't know how to stay and make it better, but they also don't know how to leave the relationship either. So they remain unhappy and paralyzed with indecision. They complain to their girlfriends about their husbands, maybe drinking too much wine, spending too much money, or spending far too much time distracting themselves with flirtations on social media so they don't actually have to think about the fact that they are both unhappy and stuck. They numb themselves so they don't ever have to face the reality of their lives head-on. So, of course, nothing ever really changes one way or the other. The relationship never feels good, but at the same time, they do not leave for something else that would make them feel better. Here's why:

I've Tried Everything: We tell ourselves that we've tried everything we can to make the relationship better and nothing has worked. But you would probably also agree with me that we've had zero training and have not been equipped with the tools to be successful. Let's say I set out to write a book and thought to myself, "It should be easy enough. Just type in about 50,000 words into a computer. How difficult can that be?" That's the equivalent of what we do when we enter into a long-term relationship. We think to ourselves, "We love each other. We said we would stay together forever. How difficult can it be?"

You and I both know there's so much more to writing a book than just finding 50,000 random words and typing them into Microsoft Word. You have to know who you're speaking to and what their problem is (in their specific words). You have to have an outline and path through the pain to actually be able to help them with their problem, otherwise you're wasting their time, and they won't get past page three. You have to be clear about how you want them to be different by the end of the book. Oh, and then, you have to know how to get it published, and into the hands of the people who have the problem you help solve. *Easy enough, right?* (Did you know 90% of people say they want to write a book but most never do?)

Likewise, being in relationship with the same person is not for the faint of heart. And we've gone into this without any training, tools, or even role-models to help do this well – particularly when things get difficult. In my opinion, this is like asking someone to write a book in English who barely speaks the language. It's going to be painful for the author – and the reader.

I know for sure that, at this point, you haven't tried everything. You might have tried everything you know, but what about all the tools that you don't know? What about the concepts that have worked for thousands of people, but sadly no one taught you how to implement? You may have tried what you know, but most of us know precious little about how to create and sustain a relationship over the course of a lifetime.

Failing in Advance: Sometimes people have given up before they even start. They determine up front that it's not going to work, and they tell themselves, "I've heard it all before, my relationship is different. This won't work for me." Unfortunately, these people won't ever really try to solve their problem. They will tell themselves they're trying because they're buying books and courses and reading every online article they can find, but they're not doing what's required to solve the problem. Instead, they choose to not ever try so they won't ever fail...which is really just a way of failing in advance.

This Is a Pain You Know: You've woken up feeling this way for months, years, maybe even decades. It doesn't feel good, but it certainly feels better than walking through the unknown of leaving and starting over, or even opening your heart to your husband again to give it yet another try. Remaining where you are, stuck, frustrated, and unhappy, although not optimal, is a pain that you know how to exist within and doesn't require you to take any new action that feels incredibly uncomfortable. In a way, remaining in the place of being stuck might actually serve you.

You're Believing Your Own Bullshit: I hear from literally more than 3,000 women each month who are unhappy in their marriages and want an answer for themselves to the stay or go question. And yet, there are only seven or eight women each month that really take that step to invest in themselves and get serious about solving the issue for themselves. That's less than .003% that are serious about getting clarity. Why is that? They don't actually want to solve the problem, and unfortunately they're believing their own bullshit stories.

Hear me out: I know...I know. You're saying to yourself, "I want clarity, Sharon, but I can't afford to work with you." I'm going to say this bluntly on purpose to get your attention. That story you've created is bullshit and believing that excuse only serves to keep you stuck in pain longer. Here's how I know that: Let's say you live in the snow belt of Cleveland, Ohio, and it's the dead of winter. Your furnace breaks down and the repairman says it's not salvageable and needs to be completely replaced. You don't have the money to replace the entire furnace that costs thousands of dollars. But somehow you find the money, don't you? You're not going to stay in a home when it is two degrees Fahrenheit outside, letting your pipes burst, and your kids freeze to death. You figure it out because it's a priority. I know this because I had to do this myself two winters ago. This is no different. You have simply told yourself the story that it's optional. If your pipes were going to burst, and in the next two months, you and the kids were going to freeze to death if you didn't get an answer for yourself about your marriage, you would figure it out. You would. We all would. I did. If 3,000 furnaces needed to be replaced in Cleveland, Ohio, in the dead of winter, you cannot tell me that only eight people would choose to replace their furnaces so that they could have heat. The primitive brain loves having you believe the bullshit story it's created for you (*you can't afford to solve this problem*). As long as you believe that story, you permit yourself to keep the story about having tried everything, to keep the pain you know, and to not have to take any scary action. My friend, that story is keeping you stuck and locked in a prison of your own making...and you're the only one with the key.

Clarity Isn't Just for the Few and the Lucky

You might think that real clarity – an answer that you have peace with, an answer that you trust, and can take action on – is only for the few and the lucky. That's not true. It's a choice to make clarity in your most important, most intimate relationship a priority.

I met a woman whom I'll refer to as Julianne on a Thursday morning during one of my Truth & Clarity sessions. These are complimentary sessions I hold with people to understand where they're struggling and whether or not there's a fit for us to work together. She would have to feel comfortable with me so that I can get her to where she's wanting to go. I would have to feel like I can genuinely help her and that she's coachable and ready for this level of clarity (as we've discussed, not everyone is...). I'll be honest, when I spoke with Julianne for the first time, I wasn't sure I could help her. You see, she had a lot to say about all the changes her husband needed to make which would make her happy. She seemed pretty tied to him needing to change. The problem was that she was the one wanting change and the one I was talking to. I took a chance and took her on as a client, not knowing for sure whether or not she would be coachable. Three weeks into applying the tools I taught her – only a fraction of what I've shared with you in this book – here's what she had to say:

"Working with Sharon has completely changed my marriage. After twenty-two years of struggling to understand each other and [being] on the brink of divorce, she taught me how to do things differently and in turn, saved my marriage (and my sanity).

I was very skeptical of hiring a life coach, at first thinking I knew everything and [that] it was my husband who needed to change. But in only three sessions, she completely changed my perspective and I am more in love with my husband than ever before. Best thing I ever did!"

Again, with the same tools, same teaching material, same teacher, some people are more in love than ever before, while others tell me they've "been there, done that, didn't work."

And then there was Deanna, who told me how she has known for three years that her answer is to leave her marriage. She was tired of trying, and although she had love for the man who is the father of her children, she is no longer in love with him. Three years ago, she told him she wanted to separate, and yet here she was, still living under the same roof, ignoring the same issues, only to have more resentments mounted on top of those she felt years ago. Two months after working with me and applying my tools, Deanna and her husband were officially separated, finding their way through their new realities. They had a separation agreement in place and were close to knowing what the dissolution of their marriage would look like, without hating one another in the process.

Her sister, by stark contrast, went through a divorce two years prior where they spent $130,000 in lawyers to battle and argue about their stuff because no one had ever equipped either of them to behave like emotional adults. That money was the college fund for one of their children and now it was being spent on lawyers because two people who once pledged to love each other forever couldn't communicate to save their lives or their life savings. Now, imagine how their children will have to navigate every single family event in the future: every graduation, every wedding, every holiday, and every grandchild's birthday party. Even if the decision is that the relationship is complete and should end, that doesn't mean the only way to do so is to spew anger, venom, and hate at one another, spending tens or hundreds of thousands of dollars in the process.

Managing the Drama

My publisher and business coach, Angela Lauria, is a very wise women and she's been in my life (and my head) for about five years. I often hear her voice in the back of my mind when I'm struggling in indecision myself. She would often say to me: "Sharon, there's the real issue and then there's drama." Some things are real issues: Children attempting to hurt themselves or someone else, physical pain in the body, losing your home, being addicted to drugs, and someone you love either getting sick or passing. Those are real issues that require real solutions. Almost everything else is some version of drama that we create in our minds, begin to believe, and use as an excuse to keep us from every single thing we really want in our lives. Challenge yourself. Hear my voice in the back of your mind, asking you: "Is this a real issue or is this drama?"

Everything I've taught you in this book can help you manage that drama so that you can actually create a life and come to a decision that feels like home.

There Is No Wrong Answer

In the question of whether to stay or go, I truly believe there is no wrong answer – except of course, choosing to not answer the question for yourself. At the beginning of this book I told you that most people think they have two options:

1. Stay and remain unhappy
2. Blow up their lives and leave the marriage

I also told you that I present clients with two much better options:

1. Stay, recommit, and reconnect so the relationship evolves into something new and feels good for both of you
2. Lovingly release the relationship and move forward without regret

Now, I'm going to consolidate this into the three options you're faced with:

1. Stay and evolve the relationship into a 2.0 version that looks and feels dramatically different than what it's been historically
2. Stay and remain unhappy, constantly complaining and wishing the marriage could be different than it actually is but never taking any action to either make it better or leave the marriage
3. Lovingly, gently release the relationship, moving forward without anger or regret

Given those options, the only wrong answer is Option 2 – choosing not to decide one way or the other and remaining unhappy and miserable. Even though you're not making a choice between stay or go, you still are making a choice. It's making the choice to remain stuck.

I want answers for you. I want you to honestly and consciously choose either Option 1 or Option 3. I want you to refuse to choose Option 2, no matter what your primitive mind says. I want you to pull yourself out of the place where it all feels so empty, lonely, and stuck. I want you to feel hopeful again about what's ahead of you. Option 1 allows you to create the next version of your relationship that feels good for both of you, a new version that has never existed before. It allows you to release all the expectations so that you can love freely. Option 3 allows you to walk away in love, compassion, and kindness, without harboring decades of guilt or resentment. Either are perfectly valid options for you to step into a life that feels like home.

I have no agenda here in your life. There are people who want to stay in their marriage and there are people that want to leave the marriage. I honor either choice. The choice I cannot honor is choosing to remain stuck in indecision and unhappiness. As a coach, I had to learn a long time ago that I could not help or save everybody. There is no human being on the planet that could actually save the 3,000 people that reach out to me each month. (I'm pretty magical, but not that magical.) Therefore, I had to focus on those that were willing to step forward for themselves and be ready for real clarity in their lives and marriages.

You've walked with me this far.

There must be some nugget of goodness in here that spoke to you which will help move you closer to clarity.

And there will be a portion of you that will want me to take you by the hand and guide you personally through this to your answer for your heart, for your marriage, for your life.

If that's you, here's where you can find out more about my coaching and how to take that next step if you feel like you're ready for that level of clarity: https://www.clarityformymarriage.com.

Work with Me

To learn more about working with Sharon directly to help you navigate this difficult decision for your heart and your marriage, go to:

www.ClarityforMyMarriage.com

ACKNOWLEDGEMENTS

T hank you to my amazing clients who have trusted me with the most intimate parts of their lives. You inspire me and challenge me in all the very best ways. I have so much love and gratitude for each of you.

Thank you to Traci Snyder for your encouragement, inspiration, and deep belief in me. You make me laugh. You make me stretch myself. With you, I always know I am understood and loved. You are powerful beyond measure, my soul sister.

Thank you to Angela Lauria and the team at The Author Incubator. Now seven books later, we've done some incredible things together. Thank you for always telling me the truth and having my back.

Thank you to my sweet Mama and Dad for showing me what an abiding, devoted love looks like for more than 50 years.

Thank you to Madison, Shannon, Rick, Pam, and Jonathon for all the ways you make this work like a well-oiled machine. I'm so lucky to work with such exceptional human beings to create an extraordinary business. I appreciate you so much!

And thank you to D. for everything always. You are the wind at my back that helps propel me forward and I am grateful for each day that I get to love you.

ABOUT THE AUTHOR

Sharon is a certified Master Life Coach and six-time #1 international bestselling author on love and relationships. She is the relationship coach for when you are struggling in a lonely and disconnected marriage, seeking confidence and clarity so you can either fix your marriage or move forward without regret. Her work has been widely published, including features in the *New York Times*, mindbodygreen, HuffPost, Thrive Global, and MSN.com.

Sharon trained as a coach under Martha Beck, PhD. Prior to coaching, she was a marketing executive for twenty years. She holds an undergraduate degree from Ohio University and an MBA from Ashland University.

The loves of her life are her husband, Derrick, and their two pups, Leo and Luna. She has recently relocated from the Midwest to Florida to live out their dream of being near the water.

Connect with Sharon online:

Web Site: www.sharonpopetruth.com

Blog: www.sharonpopetruth.com/blog-featured-posts

YouTube: SharonPopeOnYouTube

Twitter: @SharonPopeTruth

Facebook: www.facebook.com/SharonPopeTruthCoach

LinkedIn: www.linkedin.com/pub/sharon-pope/8/5b2/70

Instagram: www.instagram.com/sharonpopetruth

Pinterest: www.pinterest.com/sharonpopetruth

ABOUT DIFFERENCE PRESS

Difference Press is the exclusive publishing arm of The Author Incubator, an educational company for entrepreneurs – including life coaches, healers, consultants, and community leaders – looking for a comprehensive solution to get their books written, published, and promoted. Its founder, Dr. Angela Lauria, has been bringing to life the literary ventures of hundreds of authors-in-transformation since 1994.

A boutique-style self-publishing service for clients of The Author Incubator, Difference Press boasts a fair and easy-to-understand profit structure, low-priced author copies, and author-friendly contract terms. Most importantly, all of our #incubatedauthors maintain ownership of their copyright at all times.

Let's Start a Movement with Your Message

In a market where hundreds of thousands of books are published every year and are never heard from again, The Author Incubator is different. Not only do all Difference Press books reach Amazon bestseller status, but all of our authors are actively changing lives and making a difference.

Since launching in 2013, we've served over 500 authors who came to us with an idea for a book and were able to write it and get it self-published in less than 6 months. In addition, more than 100 of those books were picked up by traditional publishers and are now available in book stores. We do this by selecting the highest quality and highest potential applicants for our future programs.

Our program doesn't only teach you how to write a book – our team of coaches, developmental editors, copy editors, art directors, and marketing experts incubate you from having a book idea to being a published, bestselling author, ensuring that the book you create can actually make a difference in the world. Then we give you the training you need to use your book to make the difference in the world, or to create a business out of serving your readers.

Are You Ready to Make a Difference?

You've seen other people make a difference with a book. Now it's your turn. If you are ready to stop watching and start taking massive action, go to http://theauthorincubator.com/apply/.

"Yes, I'm ready!"

DIFFERENCE
P R E S S

OTHER BOOKS BY DIFFERENCE PRESS

Small Town Divorce: A Road Map through Devastation, Despair, and Drama by Denise J. Anderson

To Medicate or Not? That Is the Question: The Ultimate Guide to Improving Blood Test Results by Asha Pai Bohannon, PharmD, CDE, CPT

Solve Your Sleep for Better Health: Get to the Core of Your Snore by Amy Dayries-Ling, DMD, FAIHM

Help! My Teen Has Diabetes: The Resource for Frustrated Parents by Hadea Fisher

Holy Sh*t, My Kid Is Cutting!: The Complete Plan To Stop Self-Harm by J.J. Kelly, Psy.D.

The Ultimate Cure for Depression: Leveraging Science and Faith for Total Healing by Joy Kwakuyi

Skyrocket Your Business at Zero Cost: Make the Difference in Company Growth and Community Development by Dr. Francis N. Mbunya

The High School Sweetheart's Survival Guide to Uncoupling: Secrets to Moving Forward after a Marriage That Defined You by Karinne Piat

Transform Yourself Through Disease: 8 Steps to Reclaim Your Health and Your Life by Rory Reich

PTSD and a Drug-Free Me: Get Real about Handling Trauma without Abusing Drugs, Alcohol, or Prescription Meds by Catherine Scherwenka

Oh My Gosh, My Child Wants to Be an Actor: The Art of Raising an Artist by Lilia Sixtos

This Is Not 'The End': Strategies to Get Through the Worst Chapters of Your Life by Nina Sossoman-Pogue

Broken Stronger: 8 Non-Negotiable Steps to Break Free and Become Your Own Boss by Elena Zehr

Work with Me

To learn more about working with Sharon
directly to help you navigate this difficult
decision for your heart and your marriage, go to:

www.ClarityforMyMarriage.com